M000268031

Japanese Textiles

IN THE VICTORIA AND ALBERT MUSEUM

JAPANESE TEXTILES
IN THE VICTORIA AND ALBERT MUSEUM

ANNA JACKSON

PHOTOGRAPHS BY IAN THOMAS

V&A PUBLICATIONS

First published by V&A Publications, 2000

V&A Publications
160 Brompton Road
London SW3 1HW

© The Board of Trustees of the Victoria and Albert Museum, 2000

Anna Jackson asserts her moral right to be identified as the author
of this book

Designed by Cara Gallardo, Area

ISBN 978 1 851 77317 6
Library of Congress Control Number 2008922743

10 9 8 7 6 5 4 3 2
2011 2010 2009 2008

A catalogue record for this book is available from the
British Library.

All rights reserved. No part of this publication may be reproduced,
stored in a retrieval system, or transmitted in any form or by any
means electronic, mechanical, photocopying, recording or
otherwise, without written permission of the Publishers.

Printed in Singapore by Imago

Photography by Ian Thomas, V&A Photographic Studio

Every effort has been made to seek permission to reproduce those
images whose copyright does not reside with the V&A, and we are
grateful to the individuals and institutions who have assisted in this
task. Any omissions are entirely unintentional, and the details
should be addressed to the Publishers

COVER ILLUSTRATIONS

Front: *Kimono* (detail, Plate 95)
Back: Gift cover (*fukusa*, detail, Plate 134)
Frontispiece: Map of Japan, showing major textile regions

V&A Publications
160 Brompton Road
London SW3 1HW
www.vam.ac.uk

Contents

ACKNOWLEDGEMENTS

I would like to thank my colleagues Verity Wilson for her enormous help and encouragement and for the many hours she spent helping me to grasp the complexities of weaving, Rupert Faulkner for his careful reading of the text, and Ian Thomas for taking the fabulous photographs. I would also like to thank Julia Gray for sharing with me her knowledge of Japanese embroidery skills.

NOTES ON JAPANESE NAMES AND PRONUNCIATION

Japanese names are given in the Japanese order: family name followed by given name. Japanese terms are italicised throughout.

Consonants in Japanese are pronounced in much the same way as they are in English, the vowels as they are in Italian. There is a difference, however, between the long and short u/ū and o/ō, the macron over the vowel indicating the longer form. The shorter form 'u' is pronounced as in 'cruet', the longer form 'ū' as in 'boot'; the shorter form 'o' as in 'hot', the longer form 'ō' as in 'oar'. Macrons have been used throughout the text except on the frequently found place names such as Tokyo, Kyoto, Osaka (strictly speaking Tōkyō, Kyōto and Ōsaka).

INTRODUCTION

The collection of Japanese textiles at the Victoria and Albert Museum numbers over 1,300 pieces dating from the seventeenth century to the present day. It includes garments that would have been worn by Japan's wealthy urban elite, by members of the court, by actors, by Buddhist priests and by those living in rural areas. As well as items of dress, the collection includes textiles that would have covered ceremonial gifts and decorated temples, and domestic items such as bedding covers. Much of the collection is in the form of fabric lengths and small samples. This reflects the Museum's preoccupation, particularly in the late nineteenth century, with the acquisition of objects that would serve as examples of different kinds of decorative techniques. The survival of these fabric samples also demonstrates the way in which the textile arts have been valued in Japan. Many of the examples have been mounted in albums by those involved in textile manufacture, or by textile collectors, as a means of recording and circulating information. This group of objects includes sample books produced by dye houses, weaving workshops and textile merchants to promote their products.

The V&A acquired its first group of Japanese textiles in 1865 in the form of a gift from Queen Victoria (see plates 5, 6 and 30). These were part of a large group of objects of various media received by the Queen from one of the last *shōgun* to mark the diplomatic and commercial treaty signed by Britain and Japan in 1858. The opening of Japan to western powers in the 1850s caused a craze for all things Japanese and an enormous quantity of goods began to be imported into Britain. The Museum purchased Japanese textiles from specialist dealers (see plates 44–6) and from shops such as Liberty's in Regent Street (see plate 94). It also acquired textiles from the Japanese displays at various international exhibitions (see plates 56, 57, 97, 145, 146 and 150). The Museum also benefited from private collectors such as Robert Forrer (see plates 11 and 65) and Sydney Vacher (see plate 16) who sold or gave parts of their collection to the V&A. The Museum's greatest Japanese textile benefactor was TB Clark-Thornhill, who served in the British diplomatic corps in Japan in the late nineteenth century (see plates 4, 7, 8, 17–20, 24, 32–40, 123, 129, 130 and 137–9). Most of the objects that reached the West from Japan at this time were contemporary pieces made specifically for the export market. Those who, like Clark-Thornhill, were able to travel to Japan had the opportunity to acquire items such as Buddhist textiles that were not yet readily available in the West.

Throughout the twentieth century the V&A continued to acquire textiles from the collections of private individuals (see plate 14) and from those, or the families of those, who brought items back from Japan in the late nineteenth and early twentieth centuries (see plates 26, 98, 122, 125, 132 and 143). In 1963, for example, the Museum acquired a group of gift covers (*fukusa*) from a Mrs Farmer, who had lived in Japan as a young girl when her father was working there as a tea merchant (see plate 134). According to a letter in the V&A's archive, 'the Emperor of Japan had never seen a white child and sent for her ... Following the visit he sent a royal procession to her home with gifts. Her mother ... not knowing Japanese custom [see page 16], kept the fucsas [sic] instead of returning them as she should have done. An embarrassed father tried to return them to the palace, but was told by the emperor to keep them.'

The Museum has also widened the range of Japanese textiles in its collection. In the 1950s and 1960s the V&A became one of the first museums in the West to collect Japanese folk (*mingei*) textiles, these being acquired for the Museum by Jaap Langewis, a Dutch anthropologist working in Japan (see plates 48–54, 78, 79 and 81–4). In 1970 the Museum's Japanese textiles, previously held by the Textile and Dress Department, were transferred to the newly formed Far Eastern Department. Since that time the department has built on the existing collection, focusing particularly on items of dress and, more recently, on contemporary works. Many of these pieces have been acquired from dealers in Japan and the USA or, in the case of newer pieces, from the artists themselves.

Over its long history the Museum has, inevitably, not followed any one consistent acquisition policy. Japanese textiles often entered the collection as much by serendipity as by design, and acquisitions frequently reflect the interests of a particular time as well as of individual curators. Although varied, the collection is thus, by its very nature, far from comprehensive. It is therefore not feasible, nor desirable, to present a complete history of Japanese textiles in this publication. With no early material and a predominance of nineteenth- and early twentieth-century pieces a chronological approach to the objects would not be particularly informative. Instead the objects have been arranged according to whether their primary decorative appearance derives from weaving, dyeing, embroidery or stitching techniques. The following essay is designed to give a brief overview of the kinds of textiles in the V&A, but the majority of the book is devoted to detailed illustrations of the objects themselves, many of which have never been published before.

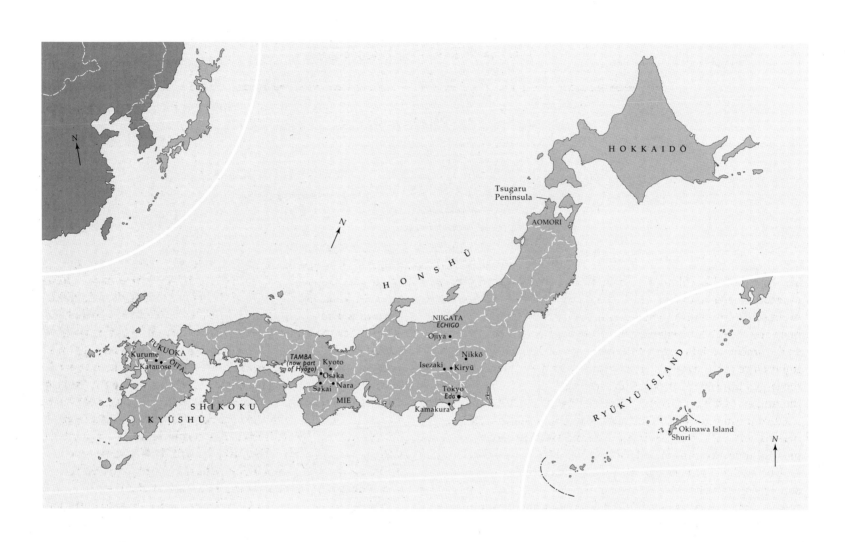

HOKKAIDŌ

Tsugaru
Peninsula

HONSHŪ

AOMORI

NIIGATA
ÉCHIGO

Ojiya •

Nikkō •
Isezaki • • Kiryū

FUKUOKA
Kurume • • OITA
Katanose •

TAMBA
(now part
of Hyōgo)
Kyoto •
• Osaka
Sakai • • Nara
MIE

Tokyo
Edo •

Kamakura •

SHIKOKU

KYŪSHŪ

RYŪKYŪ ISLAND

Okinawa Island
Shuri

N

Japanese Textiles

Anna Jackson

The textile arts have played a prominent part in the cultural history of Japan. The Japanese mastery of a wide variety of weaving, dyeing and embroidery techniques has led to the creation of a rich body of wonderfully designed and decorated textiles. Many of these skills came to Japan from the Asian mainland. Of particular importance in the early history of Japanese textile production were the large numbers of artisans who came from China and Korea in the fifth and sixth century AD. Large quantities of silk cloth also reached Japan throughout the Asuka (593–710) and Nara (710–94) periods, and such imported knowledge and examples proved a great stimulus to domestic production.

During the Nara period textile production came under central supervision with the establishment of the Weaving Office (*Oribe no tsukasa*), which was responsible for the weaving and dyeing of textiles for the imperial court. Many of the textiles worn at court were imported or produced by Chinese and Korean weavers. Silk cloth was also woven in the provinces and sent to the capital in the form of tribute or tax. In order to improve the quality of this silk, the Weaving Office sent skilled artisans to the provinces to teach weaving techniques.

In 794 the capital moved from Nara to Heian-kyo, or Kyoto as it is now known. For the next thousand years Kyoto remained the home of the imperial court and the centre of the luxury textile industry. During the Heian period (794–1185) the centralised bureaucracy that controlled textile production began to break down as powerful families started to employ their own private weavers. Relations with China had been terminated at the end of the ninth century, but were re-established during the last years of the Heian period. Again textiles were an important and much sought after

import, and domestic weavers began to copy Chinese fabrics. During the Kamakura period (1185–1336) Japan came under the rule of the warrior *samurai* class.[1] The military elite provided a new market for textile artisans, who began to break away from their patrons and establish guilds. Cloth markets also began to be held in major towns, and this encouraged the growth of textile merchants and brokers.

In the fourteenth century military power passed to the Ashikaga clan, who ruled from Muromachi in Kyoto. Although an important era culturally, the Muromachi period (1336–1573) was a time of internal chaos. The breakdown of political administration led to the Onin Wars (1467–77), which left Kyoto totally devastated. The textile artisans were among those who fled the city, seeking refuge at Buddhist temples or patronage in the towns of powerful provincial lords. Many weavers went to Sakai, a thriving port near present-day Osaka. Here they came into contact with the newest textile imports from China, which enabled them to study techniques such as the use of applied metal foil (*surihaku*) and metallic paper strips (*kinran* and *ginran*), and the weaving of crêpe (*chirimen*) and monochrome figured satins (*rinzu*).

The Momoyama period (1573–1603) saw the unification of Japan by three great military leaders: Oda Nobunaga (1534–82), Toyotomi Hideyoshi (1536–98) and Tokugawa Ieyasu (1542–1616). Although a turbulent period of Japanese history, this was also an era of great luxury when the textile arts flourished. Portuguese and later Dutch traders brought exotic textiles such as velvet, wool and printed fabrics to Japan. When Kyoto was rebuilt the weavers returned, settling in Nishijin, a former military camp on the western side of the imperial palace. The country was finally unified in the early seventeenth century and Tokugawa Ieyasu became *shōgun* (military leader).[2] He chose as his capital Edo, a small town several hundred miles to the north-east of the old centre of power. Edo grew to be an enormous city and by 1720 had over a million inhabitants. Some textile artisans moved there to profit from the opportunities this new centre of consumption had to offer. However, the old capital, Kyoto, continued to be the centre of luxury textile production.

The Edo period (1603–1868) was a time of unprecedented peace and prosperity. As the country thrived so did Nishijin and by the end of the seventeenth century there were over 7,000 looms in operation. The textile industry supported an extensive network of artisans including spinners, weavers, dyers, embroiderers, stencil makers, metallic thread suppliers and designers. At the heart of the industry were the drapery stores, which catered for a new kind of customer – the wealthy commoner. The increased demand for goods and the introduction of a cash economy brought riches to many of the merchant class, but the strict social hierarchy of Tokugawa rule prevented them from using their affluence to gain political power. Instead they used their money to acquire luxury goods such as sumptuous clothing. Nishijin continued to cater for established patrons such as the imperial court, Buddhist temples and the *Nō* theatre (see page 12), as well as for the ruling *samurai* class, but it was the fashion-conscious merchant classes who most stimulated further developments in the textile arts, particularly through their demand for new and exciting garment designs.

Nishijin suffered a number of disasters in the eighteenth century. A great fire in 1730 destroyed an estimated 3,000 looms and caused a large number of weavers to move to the provincial areas. Another fire in 1788 had a similar effect. As the Edo period progressed Nishijin was further challenged. Conspicuous displays of wealth by the merchant classes seriously threatened the social order and periodically the shogunate passed sumptuary laws designed to curb such ostentatious behaviour. These regulations often focused on issues of dress, restricting the wearing of silk and the use of particular patterning techniques by the commoner classes. Such laws – and in particular the Tempō reforms of 1830–44, which outlawed locally based guilds – had an adverse affect on Nishijin business.

Another challenge came from competition from regional textile centres that thrived under the patronage of local *daimyō* (provincial lords). Kiryu, for example, became an effective rival to Nishijin in the nineteenth century as it was nearer to the main silk producing areas and to the great market of Edo. Domestic sericulture expanded greatly in the Edo period and with it provincial spinning and weaving. Cotton, which had been introduced in the sixteenth century, also had a dramatic effect on textile manufacture and trade. Many farmers began not only to grow this very profitable crop, but to process it as well. By the beginning of the nineteenth century rural producers were able to compete with urban artisans and merchants in the supply of finished goods.

Nishijin was dealt a further blow in the second half of the nineteenth century. In 1853 an American naval squadron arrived off the coast of Japan demanding that the country open its ports to foreign power.[3] This external threat, coupled with growing internal unrest, led to the overthrow of shogunal power and the restoration of the emperor in 1868. The imperial capital moved to Tokyo, depriving Kyoto of its longest-standing patron. The establishment of Shintō as the state religion led to the destruction of temples and a decline in the demand for Buddhist vestments. The abolition of the *samurai* deprived the *Nō* theatre of its patrons, and production of robes fell severely as a consequence.

After an initial decline, however, Nishijin recovered by embracing rather than rejecting the new order. In 1872 five weavers were sent to the major silk weaving centre of Lyon, France, to learn about western production. The jacquard loom they brought back to Japan revolutionised Nishijin weaving practices. Chemical dyes were introduced and, in 1876, a series of western books on spinning, weaving and dyeing were translated into Japanese. Textile production was also stimulated by the furnishing of the new Imperial Palace in Tokyo and by a series of national exhibitions held for the encouragement of domestic industry. The Meiji period (1868–1912) government was keen for Japan to take its place on the world stage and the country was a major contributor to International Exhibitions held in Europe and the USA. The woven, dyed and embroidered fabrics fascinated visitors to these exhibitions and helped to create new markets for Japanese textiles.

The introduction of western science and technology in Japan speeded up textile production, lowered costs and provided textile designers with the opportunity to create striking new patterns. These developments reached a peak in the Taisho period (1912–26), an age of political democratisation, economic prosperity and cultural expansiveness. At the turn of the century old textile merchants such as Mitsukoshi and Takashimaya had transformed themselves into modern department stores, and it was these stores that encouraged and promoted the new textile designs. Such developments continued into the Showa period (1926–89), though they were to be short-lived.

The turmoil of the Second World War caused great damage to all aspects of cultural life in Japan. There was a shortage of material and labour, and in 1940 laws were passed that limited the production of luxury goods. The war brought irrevocable changes to the Japanese textile industry. The wearing of Japanese style dress and the use of other traditional textiles severely declined in the post-war era. However, the physical and psychological trauma of the war and the subsequent American occupation led to a national surge of interest in Japan's artistic heritage. In the 1950s various laws were passed to protect cultural properties. These laws covered not only buildings but also practices and those who engaged in them. The latter, known as Important Intangible Cultural Properties or, more commonly, Living National Treasures, included a number of textile artists. Japan also embraced and pioneered advanced technological innovations and today produces some of the most diverse and exciting textiles in the world.

Woven Patterns

The fabric woven for the use of Japan's social and economic elite was made from silk, which has been cultivated in Japan since the third century AD. Textiles used by the lower echelons of society were traditionally made from fibres gathered from wild plants.[4] Such 'bast fibres' were known as *asa* in Japan, a term most commonly used to describe the grass fibres hemp and ramie that were produced from specially cultivated plants. These fibres produced a fabric that was softer, and more expensive, than that of other bast fibres and was often used to make summer garments (see plates 53, 54, 87–9 and 103). Other cloth woven with bast fibres include elm-bark fibre (*ohyō*) woven in Hokkaidō by the Ainu, Japan's indigenous people (see plate 149), and banana fibre (*bashō*) woven in the Ryūkyū Islands, the archipelago that stretches to the south of Japan and which was, until the late nineteenth century, an independent kingdom (see plate 80). The introduction of cotton, which was soft, warm and comfortable to wear, transformed the clothing and domestic textiles of the populace (see plates 1, 2, 50–2, 75–7 and 81–6).[5] Extensive trade in cotton, whether as thread or as finished cloth, meant that it was used even in areas where it was not cultivated.

The majority of cotton and *asa* cloth is woven in plain weave (*hira-ori*), as is much silk fabric (see plates 3, 55, 91, 92, 99, 111, 116, 118 and 145). In this, the simplest weave structure, the weft (horizontal) thread passes over and under each successive warp (vertical) thread, each row reversing the order of the one before. Silk crêpe (*chirimen*), introduced into Japan from China in the sixteenth century, is also a plain weave, but has a crimped surface that is produced by over-twisting the weft threads (see plates 66, 69, 95–8, 100–2, 106, 108 and 112).

Twill (*aya*) has been woven in Japan since the Nara period. In twill weave the weft passes over or under two or more warps, creating what is known as a float. Each passage of the weft starts one place to the right or left of the previous one, creating a diagonal movement across the fabric. Satin (*shu*) is also a float weave. Long floats are created by passing the weft over or under four or more warps, giving the fabric a lustrous appearance (see plates 121–6 and 128–35).

In float weaves the surface of the fabric can show either predominantly warps or predominantly wefts depending on the weaving sequence. Figured fabrics, such as figured twill (*mon aya*, see plate 4), are woven by using different combinations of warp and weft floats to create patterns. The most common of such figured fabrics in Japan is *rinzu*, a patterned satin similar to damask, that was introduced into Japan from China in the sixteenth century (see plates 5, 6, 65, 67, 68, 70–2, 93, 94, 105, 107, 113 and 120).[6] It was produced in Japan from the early seventeenth century and gradually replaced the stiffer silks used previously. *Rinzu* was a popular fabric for *kimono*, the T-shaped garment that, from the early sixteenth century, was the principle form of dress for both sexes and all classes. Only the wealthy could afford to wear this luxury fabric however. Most *rinzu* is woven with a key-fret and small flower pattern known as *sayagata* (see plate 5 for example) but in the nineteenth century it was woven with larger patterns (see plates 6 and 120). *Mon aya* and *rinzu* are both monochrome fabrics. Other visual effects are produced when figured twill and satin are woven with warps and wefts of different colours (see plates 7–9).

Gauze has been woven in Japan since the Nara period and is particularly used for imperial garments (see plate 10). The basic weave structure, called *sha* in Japan, involves the crossing of adjacent warp threads after the insertion of each weft to form an open, but strong, structure. Variations to this structure allow for a variety of woven patterns often of great complexity. *Ro* gauze, another fabric introduced to Japan in the sixteenth century, combines plain and gauze weave to produce a softer fabric characterised by strips of densely woven material separated by rows of open weave (see plate 90).

An enormous diversity of patterns can be achieved by weaving with two or more complementary sets of warps and/or wefts or by introducing supplementary patterning threads in the warp and/or weft (see plates 11–39). Nishijin is particularly famed for its production of *nishiki*. This term is generally translated as brocade, but is actually used to describe a wide variety of silk fabrics woven with supplementary patterning warps or, more commonly, wefts of polychrome silk or metallic threads. These figure threads can be continuous, extending from edge to edge and coming to the surface where the pattern requires it, or discontinuous, extending only across the width of the pattern area.[7] *Nishiki* silks have been used for a variety of purposes. *Kimono* made from such fabrics are rare as sumptuary laws restricted their use, although the V&A has two examples from the Meiji period when such laws were no longer enforced (see plates 17 and 18). No restrictions were placed on the cloth used for *obi*, the sash that secures the *kimono*, and these polychrome fabrics were very popular (see plates 19–21). Richly woven figured silk was also used for fan cases and book covers and was an important feature of *samurai* armour (see plates 22–4).

What makes many of these woven fabrics so spectacular is the use of supplementary wefts of gold or silver. These threads are made from thinly hammered metal sheets pasted onto paper and then cut into thin strips. Monochrome fabrics woven with gold and silver strips are called *kinran* and *ginran* respectively. *Kinran* was often used in *Nō* costumes (see plates 25 and 26). *Nō* theatre first flowered in the fourteenth century and early costumes reflected those worn in real life. From the early Edo period costumes for particular roles were specially made in Nishijin. The heavy, stiff costumes, with their emphatic designs, suited the slow, deliberate movements of the *Nō* performance, which took place on an unlit and virtually bare stage. *Nō* theatre was reserved almost exclusively for the military elite and regional lords vied with each other to have the most lavishly dressed theatrical groups under their patronage.

The most elaborate of the various kinds of *Nō* robe is the *karaori* (see plate 27). This word originally meant 'Chinese weave', but like many Japanese textile terms it came to be used to describe a kind

of fabric, or in this case a garment made from the fabric, rather than a technique. *Karaori* robes, which are worn for female roles, often have three layers of simultaneously woven design: a twill weave ground (*ji*), a background geometric pattern (*jimon*) created with supplementary wefts of gold or silver, and a top pattern (*uamon*) of long floats of glossy silk that look almost like embroidery. The ground fabric is sometimes divided into blocks of alternating colours (see plate 28). *Atsuita* costumes are technically similar, but generally have bolder patterns and are used for male roles (see plate 29). Other types of costume include *kariginu* (see plate 25), which are in the form of hunting cloaks of the imperial court, and *chōken* and *maiginu*, which are fine unlined dancing cloaks.[8] These latter garments are usually made from polychrome figured gauze, but the V&A has examples of figured fabric that have a gauze-like open weave and which may have been used for such costumes (see plate 30). The comic interlude that accompanies *Nō* performances is called *Kyōgen*. Costumes were usually made from bast fibres (*asa*), although the V&A has one figured silk garment that may have been used in *Kyōgen* (see plate 31).

Many fabrics used in Buddhist temples are similar to those worn for theatrical performances. Japanese Buddhist priests wear a *kesa*, a rectangular garment that is draped over the left shoulder and under the right arm, a simple *kimono*-like garment being worn underneath (see plates 32–5). The *kesa* is made of a sewn patchwork of cloth representing a mandala, a symbolic rendering of the universe. The act of sewing is in itself a devotional pursuit, and the patchwork nature symbolises the rags of poverty. Although *kesa* sometimes utilised second-hand cloth, the technical sophistication and opulence of most examples reflect the wealth of many ecclesiastical groups.

Kesa are cut from the whole cloth and the various sections are then rearranged, often with square patches of other fabric sewn at each corner to represent the cardinal points. Some examples have an overall pictorial motif created by sewing sections of cloth side-by-side. Cord is then added to represent the usual patchwork divisions. The ground fabric sometimes has bands of different colours (see plate 35). Other figured textiles used in Buddhist temples include fabrics to adorn altars and sculptures. Like *kesa* many are woven with gold, which would have shimmered in the light of the temple candles (see plates 36–9). The V&A also has one unusual Buddhist hanging woven from human hair (see plate 40).

Another type of weaving structure used in Japan, although not well represented in the V&A's collection, is tapestry weave or *tsuzure ori* (see plates 41 and 42). This is generally a plain weave in which the warp is hidden by closely packed wefts, the latter being woven back and forth in their own pattern area rather than passing through the entire width of the fabric. The resulting fabric is characterised by solid areas of sharply defined colours.

Velvet (*birōdo*) is a pile textile produced by introducing a supplementary warp over a series of small rods. When the rods are removed the resulting loops can be cut to create the pile. In the Edo period velvet was often checked or striped (see plate 43), or woven in a single colour as the basis for richly embroidered *obi* (see plate 127). The V&A has one very unusual gift cover (*fukusa*) woven in an extremely complex, time-consuming and rarely used technique called tapestry velvet (*tsuzure birōdo*) in which extra, different coloured, pile warps create the pattern (see plate 44).[9] In the Meiji period elaborate velvet pictures were produced by first painting the image onto ready woven but uncut velvet. Some areas were then cut, producing tufted pile, while others areas were left as horizontal ridges (see plates 45–7).

The banded backgrounds seen in some *Nō* costumes and *kesa* are created by reserving large sections of warp threads. This patterning method is fundamentally the same as *kasuri*, a technique most commonly associated with the indigo-dyed fabrics produced in rural Japan (see plates 50–4), although the term would never be used to describe *Nō* and Buddhist fabrics. *Kasuri* is believed to have been introduced to Japan via the Ryūkyū Islands, where similar *ikat* techniques were imported from South-East Asia (see plates 48 and 49). Sections of yarn are tightly bound or compressed prior to being dyed. Colour does not penetrate the protected areas, creating a yarn that is partly coloured and partly white. If various colours or shades are to be used the yarns are tied and retied as necessary. The yarn is then used as the warp and/or weft so that the pattern emerges as the fabric is woven. Indigo-dyed *kasuri* cotton was used in Japan for garments and domestic items such as bedding covers (*futon-ji*, see plates 50 and 51). Summer *kimono* of *asa kasuri* were very popular in urban areas (see plate 54). After the relaxation of sumptuary laws in the Meiji period *kasuri* silk was used for *kimono* (see plate 55).

The Meiji period witnessed a great change in the weaving industry with the introduction of various mechanised loom attachments. As well as speeding up production, new technology enabled Japanese weavers to experiment with different types of cloth. The end of national isolation in Japan also gave textile artisans the chance to exhibit their skills, both old and new, to a worldwide audience. At the London International Exhibition of 1874 the Japanese showed an interesting group of open-structured plain weave fabrics (see plates 56 and 57). In one example highly twisted warps and wefts are interspersed by stripes of untwisted yarn, the differences in tension creating a puckered effect (see plate 57).

In the early twentieth century weavers and dyers in Isezaki, near Tokyo, began to use a method called *hogushiori*, 'unravel and weave', which involved printing *kasuri* patterns through stencils onto warp threads that had been woven with temporary wefts. The latter were then removed and the true wefts woven in. Sharp images were created when both warp and weft patterns were made in this way, while a combination of the new method with traditional *kasuri* techniques gave softer designs. This patterning method was popular until the Second World War (see plate 60).

Weavers in Japan today experiment with both established and experimental techniques. Shimura Fukumi (b.1924), who was made a Living National Treasure in 1990, creates plain weave checked silk in evocative shades derived from natural dyes, many of which are extracted from plants she grows herself (see plate 61). Kitamura Takeshi (b.1935) was made a Living National Treasure in 1995 for his woven gauzes. Kitamura has studied and recreated one of the earliest, and most sophisticated, gauze structures, known as *ra*, in which the members of each pair of warps are not only transposed with one another, but with adjacent pairs (see plate 62).

The twentieth century saw the increased use of manufactured fibres. Originally these were used to imitate silk, which they did very successfully; it is often difficult to distinguish between the real and the artificial (see plates 59, 106–9 and 113–15). In the second half of the century, the use of chemically made fibres allowed weavers to produce new patterns and textures. Many contemporary practitioners harness such new fabrics and new technology to create extraordinarily innovative works. *Puffed Blocks* by Arai Jun'ichi (b.1932) is, perhaps remarkably, a simple plain weave fabric (see plate 63). The elasticity and texture result purely from the exploitation of the characteristics of the different yarns. *Seaweed Scarf* by Miyamoto Eiji (b.1948) is a triple weave fabric (see plate 64). The two outer layers are of sheer fabric, while the inner has an elastic weft that interacts with the outer layers to create the pleats and shirr.

DYED PATTERNS

Most of the dyes used to colour Japanese textiles were known by the Nara period and over successive centuries their use grew more sophisticated. The origins of the various dyeing techniques used to pattern cloth can also be traced back to early periods of Japanese history. However, until the middle of the Muromachi period textiles for the elite tended to be patterned using weaving techniques. The subsequent increase in the use of dyed decorative techniques resulted from the growth of patronage. The increasing demand for luxury cloth could not be met by expensive imports from China, or by domestic production of patterned-weave cloth. There also developed a new interest in surface decoration and a desire for a freer and more graphic style, which dyed motifs – not bound by the geometry imposed by weaving – could produce. The Edo period witnessed the full development of the sophisticated dyed pictorial designs for which Japan is famous.

Some Edo period dye houses specialised in a single colour, while others dyed with a variety of colours. Although a fairly limited number of plants were used, an enormous range of colours was produced.[10] Dyeing is a very specialised skill and the top dye houses carefully guarded their secrets. Kyoto was the dye centre of Japan, but no village was without its own dye house.

The earliest Japanese textile in the V&A's collection dates from the first half of the seventeenth century (see plate 65). Like many *kimono* fabrics it is patterned with a combination of dyeing and embroidery. It also features the use of gold leaf, *surihaku*, which has been fixed to the cloth with paste applied through a stencil. The use of *surihaku*, often in combination with embroidery and tie-dyeing, against a dark ground is a feature of *kimono* from the Keichō-Kan'ei eras (1596–1644). After this time, metallic thread embroidery replaced the use of *surihaku*.

The white spotted patterns on plate 65 have been created using a technique called *shibori*, which is usually translated as tie-dyeing. This patterning method involves the binding, stitching, folding or clamping of the cloth prior to immersion in the dye. The colour does not penetrate the protected areas. The tiny 'fawn-dot' pattern is called *kanoko shibori*. In this method closely placed small circles in diagonal rows are bound tightly with thread. The tip of each tiny section of fabric is left unbound so that a small dyed dot appears in the centre of each undyed circle. After the dye is dry the bindings are carefully removed. *Kanoko shibori* was expensive and labour intensive and was usually used in combination with embroidery (see plates 66, 68 and 69). However, the V&A does have in its collection one magnificent red *kimono* which is patterned all over using the technique (see plate 67). Stitch-rest *shibori*, *nuishime shibori*, involves the outlining of areas of pattern with stitching, which is then drawn up and bound. This technique was often used to define particular areas of the design that were then generally patterned using another technique (the cloud areas in plate 69 for example). To meet the demand and reduce the cost of *kanoko shibori* a stencilled version called *kata kanoko* was introduced in the late seventeenth century (see plates 70–2).

Stencil dyeing, or *katazome*, was one of the most common methods of patterning cloth in the Edo and Meiji periods. One of the earliest stencil patterning styles to emerge was *komon*. These small dot designs were used throughout the Edo period to decorate the formal attire of *samurai* and the garments of wealthy merchants (see plates 73 and 74). From the mid Edo period a variety of larger scale stencil designs, called *chūgata*, also became popular. They were used to decorate cotton garments and household items such as bedding covers (*futon-ji*, see plates 75 and 76). Stencils are used in conjunction with rice paste which is applied through the stencil to cloth stretched out on a long board. The stencil is then removed and placed on the next section of cloth and the process repeated. When the cloth is dyed the colour does not penetrate the areas protected by the paste. Once the dye is dry the paste can be washed away. Different colours or shading can be added using other stencils or by brush. Stencils were also used to create the decorative effect of wax-resisting and block printing seen on the fabrics imported from South-East Asia during the Edo period. Both the foreign and domestic versions of this type of cloth were called *sarasa* (see plate 77).

Stencils were also used to dye the *bingata* textiles worn by members of the Ryūkyūan royalty (see plates 78 and 79). In *bingata* the dye is applied directly through the stencil onto the fabric using a stubby brush. What further distinguishes *bingata* is its brilliance of colour deriving from the use of mineral pigments. This stencil-dyeing technique was also used with indigo alone to create a fabric known as *aigata* (see plate 80).

The rice paste used in *katazome* decoration was also used to create free-hand designs. In this method, known as *tsutsugaki*, the design is drawn onto the cloth with paste squeezed from a tube (*tsutsu*, see plates 81–7). The tube is made from paper treated with persimmon juice to make it water resistant, and has a nozzle of bamboo or metal through which the paste is extruded. As with the stencil technique the paste forms a protective coating that prevents penetration of the dye. *Katazome* stencils can be used repeatedly, but the *tsutsugaki* technique produces only one piece at a time. It was often employed to produce textiles for special occasions such as weddings. One of the most important items in a bride's trousseau was the decorative cover for the *futon*, which is the traditional form of Japanese bedding (see plates 83 and 84). These would be decorated with auspicious symbols designed to bring good fortune to a newly wed couple. The bold patterns created by *tsutsugaki* were also ideal for festival banners (see plate 85) and for *noren*, the curtains that hang in the doorways of shops and restaurants to indicate that they are open for business (see plate 86).

Tsutsugaki is technically related to *yūzen*, a technique named after Miyazaki Yūzen, a late eighteenth-century artist monk traditionally credited with its invention (see plates 88–101). The two techniques are rarely discussed together, however: *tsutsugaki* was used to decorate the cotton textiles used in rural Japan while *yūzen* was used to pattern the elegant garments of the wealthy urban dwellers. A very fine nozzle is used for *yūzen*, creating a far more detailed and delicate line than in *tsutsugaki*, and the colouring is achieved through the brushing on of the various dyes rather than by immersing. However, when the free-hand paste method is used with indigo to pattern *asa* it is difficult to determine where the divide between the two techniques should be drawn (see plates 87–9).

Yūzen is often used to decorate *chirimen* crêpe, the crimped matt surface of the cloth being well suited to the detailed patterning (see plates 95–8, 100, 101, 106 and 112). However, very occasionally plain weave silk (see plates 91–2 and 99), gauze (see plate 90) and even monochrome figured satin (*rinzu*, see plates 93 and 94) is used. As *yūzen* is a free-hand method of patterning, extremely detailed and highly pictorial patterns can be produced.

Another paste-resist method that developed alongside *yūzen* was *chaya-zome*, a technique that results in an indigo blue design on a white ground (see plates 102 and 103). This involved the extensive application of paste, leaving only small areas of design to create the pattern when the cloth was dyed. This highly skilled and expensive technique was reserved for the summer *kimono* of high ranking *samurai* women.

In the second half of the nineteenth century the dyer's palette was altered by the introduction of chemical dyes. In the late 1870s a method was devised of directly applying pre-coloured paste, instead of resist-paste, through stencils. This method eliminated several stages of the *yūzen* process and encouraged the development of ever more sophisticated patterns. The stencil dye process was often used in conjunction with colour gradation techniques (see plates 100 and 101).

In the twentieth century traditional methods of dyeing, such as *shibori* and *yūzen*, have survived alongside increasingly automated methods of patterning textiles. Some decorative motifs remain very traditional in style, while others show more modern influences (see plates 104–15). Automated methods are also used to recreate the effects of traditional patterning techniques such as *komon* (see plate 114).

Many twentieth-century artists sought to preserve traditional dyeing methods within an increasingly mechanised environment. The survival of *bingata*, for example, owes much to the work of the late Tokyo-based artist Serizawa Keisuke (1895–1984). During his lifetime Serizawa, who was made a Living National Treasure in 1956, created an enormously diverse number of *bingata* dyed textiles including *kimono*, *noren* and screens (see plate 116).

A combination of *shibori* and hand-painting is employed by Furusawa Machiko (b.1933) in the creation of very lyrical textile fabrics (see plate 117), while Moriguchi Kunihiko (b.1941) uses the *yūzen* technique to produce abstract patterns based on stylised natural motifs (see plate 118). The use of traditional methods to create highly contemporary designs is also apparent in the stencil-dyed work of Matsubara Yoshichi (b.1937, see plate 119).

EMBROIDERED PATTERNS

Like other patterning methods Japanese embroidery, or *nui*, has a long history. Used to decorate clothing since the Nara period, it became very popular in the Muromachi and Momoyama periods. As with other textile arts, however, it was during the Edo period that embroidery reached its peak of technical sophistication. Exploiting the freedom of form the technique allows, and utilising a myriad of colours and a range of stitches, embroiderers have produced some of the most striking of all Japanese textiles.

Embroidery was often used in conjunction with dyeing techniques such as *shibori, katazome* and *yūzen* (see plates 65, 66 and 68–72). This combination of patterning methods gave designs a variety of textures and a sense of pattern depth.

Even when a whole pattern is created using paste-resist techniques, tiny parts of a design, such as the tips of a bird's wing, the centre of a flower or the knots on the trunk of a tree, are highlighted with embroidery (see plates 95 and 101). A variety of fabric grounds are employed, but, when embroidery is the sole decorative technique, satin is often used to give an extremely lustrous effect (see plates 121–6 and 128–35).

Japanese embroiderers employ a number of different stitches. A flat stitch (*hira-nui*), equivalent to that known as satin stitch in the West, is used to create pattern elements such as flowers and leaves. These stitches use floss (untwisted) silk, which gives the embroidery a very rich sheen. A tiny gap, equivalent to the point of the needle, is used to delineate elements such as the separate petals of flowers or the central veins of leaves (the peonies in plate 128 for example). Larger areas are defined with long and short stitches (*sashi-nui*), also in floss silk, with longer laid threads sometimes being held down with other, finer, shorter stitches (as in the body of the elephant in plate 130 for example). Long floss stitches are sometimes laid on the fabric with finer threads laid on top in a lattice (*goban-osae*). The whole pattern is held down with tiny stitches at the crossover points on the grid (the clouds in plate 138 for example). The use of small stitches to attach to the fabric threads that lie on the surface is called couching.

From the mid Edo period twisted threads began to be used. Threads are generally twisted in pairs. Depending on the effect desired this could be done lightly or tightly. For the latter, called *katayori*, one thread is highly twisted and then twisted, more lightly and in the opposite direction, with another thread. *Katayori* couched onto the fabric surface was used to outline design elements or to create a textured effect on certain areas (such as the costumes in plates 130, 131 and 134). Occasionally a whole design is created with *katayori* (see plate 135). Another type of textural effect is created with a knot stitch (*sagura-nui*, such as the elephant's eyebrows in plate 130 and the knots on the tree in plate 131).

Metallic thread was also used to great effect in Japanese embroidery. This thread is made from a silk core, wrapped in paper and then with gold or silver leaf. The thread, being thick, could not be passed through fine silk without damaging it, so was couched down, often with orange-red silk. Metallic thread embroidery is usually combined with embroidery in coloured silks, but occasionally whole, or near whole, designs are created with gold thread (see plates 132 and 133). This creates a truly dazzling effect, especially when used on a dark satin ground.

The three dimensional effect of embroidery is often enhanced with cotton or paper padding (see plates 125, 130–2, 134, 135, 138 and 140–2). The padding is attached to the fabric with a couched grid of threads or, with deeper padding, a scrim of fine fabric. The embroidery is then executed over the padding. Twisted cotton padding is sometimes couched onto the fabric to give outline to the embroidered pattern (such as the elephant in plate 130) or to create contours (such as in the old people's faces in plate 131).

The most stunning Edo period embroidery is seen not only on *kimono* and *obi*, but on gift covers called *fukusa* (see plates 129–35). Gifts were usually presented in a lacquer box placed on a tray of lacquer or wood. Over this would be placed a *fukusa*. The choice of *fukusa* appropriate to the occasion was an important part of the gift-giving ritual. The richness of the decoration was an indication of the donor's wealth and the design evidence of their taste and cultural sensitivity. After being suitably admired, the *fukusa*, along with the box and tray, would be returned to the donor. *Fukusa* gave embroiderers the ideal medium to demonstrate their powers of pictorial expression.

Embroidery was also employed to pattern textiles used in Buddhist temples and large decorative hangings (see plates 136–45). Occasionally figured silk is used as the ground for the image (see plates 136 and 137), but quite often the embroidery is executed on coarsely woven cotton and completely covers the entire surface (see plates 138–44). The embroidery between the main design elements is often used merely to create a flat pattern ground, but on some of the most spectacular hangings whole landscapes are created with embroidered stitches (see plates 141–3).

Large embroidered hangings were often bought by visitors to Japan from impoverished temples forced to sell off their belongings in the Meiji period. Realising the appeal of such items, Japanese embroiders began to produce large pictorial works aimed at the western market. Such works were also exhibited at the international exhibitions that took place in Europe and North America in the nineteenth and early twentieth centuries. The V&A purchased one such item from the Japan-Britain Exhibition held in London in 1910 (see plate 145). The pictorial nature of large hangings such as this demonstrates the close alliance between textile design and painting that existed in Japan in the Edo and Meiji periods. At the exhibitions Japan also showed off the skills of its textile workers on a much smaller scale. For the exhibition held in London in 1884 students from Kyoto Prefectural Girl's School demonstrated a variety of skills in a series of small-scale textile pictures that were mounted in an album (see plates 146 and 150).

STITCHED AND APPLIED PATTERNS

In Japan there are a number of other decorative techniques that involve the use of a needle and thread. Quilting, known as *sashiko*, is a method by which layers of fabric are sewn together with running stitch (see plate 147). Although made in various parts of Japan, *sashiko* is particularly associated with the cold north of the country. Garments stitched in this way are strong and warm and suitable for use as work apparel. In Tsugaru, the northernmost part of Honshū, locally grown hemp and ramie were woven as the base fabric for *kogin*, a stitching technique akin to *sashiko* and used to embellish *kimono* (see plate 148). In *kogin* white stitches are embroidered over and under an odd number of warps on the woven ground fabric to create a diamond pattern.

The web-like designs on Ainu textiles, which serve to protect the wearer from malevolent spirits, are created by stitching techniques (see plate 149). In the robe in the V&A's collection pieces of indigo-dyed cotton have been stitched to the elm-bark fabric using an appliqué method known as *kirifuse* (cut and lay down) and then embroidered in white cotton with a technique called *oki-nuki* (placing and sewing).

A less traditional way of applying textiles onto a fabric ground became popular in the late nineteenth century. In this relief work, *oshi-e*, pieces of fabric were wrapped around a stiff paper form and then glued to a woven ground to create pictures. Different types of woven fabric were used to create different effects, such as on the example by another student of Kyoto Prefectural Girl's School in which plain weave silk has been used for the branches and leaves and dyed crêpe silk (*chirimen*) for the soft petals (see plate 150).

NOTES

1. From 1185 until 1868 Japan was ruled by a military aristocracy. The emperor had no political power.

2. Successive heads of the Tokugawa family ruled as *shōgun* until 1868.

3. From the early seventeenth century Japan had a policy of national isolation. The Dutch were the only western country able to trade with Japan.

4. Some bast fibres were used by Japan's elite. *Kuzu* cloth, for example, was used for ceremonial *samurai* garments.

5. The examples of cotton Ryūkyūan cloth illustrated would have been worn only by elite members of society (see plates 48, 49, 78 and 79).

6. *Rinzu* is not a true damask as the structure is not reversible.

7. The use of discontinuous supplementary wefts is brocade weaving, the coloured threads being wound on bobbins and inserted into the pattern as required.

8. *Chōken* and *maiginu* costume have a different structure and the latter tends to have a move overall repeat pattern.

9. This technique is extremely rare and it is likely that this *fukusa* was made in Nishijin in the 1830s by Inoue Risuke, the only weaver known to have used this technique. See Takamura (1991), p.141.

10. See Monica Bethe. 'Color: Dyes and Pigments' in Stinchecum (1984), pp.64–6.

List of Plates

Dimensions show the length followed by the width, with garments being measured from the base of the neck to the hem and from sleeve end to sleeve end. It should be noted that no detailed technical analysis of the weave structure of these textiles has been attempted.

Plate 1
Detail of a sample
Checks
Plain weave cotton
Tamba district; 19th century
T.100F-1969
17.5 x 34 cm ($6^{7}/_{8}$ x $13^{3}/_{8}$ in)

Plate 2
Detail of a sample
Checks
Plain weave cotton
Tamba district; 19th century
T.100Q-1969
24.5 x 34 cm ($9^{5}/_{8}$ x $13^{3}/_{8}$ in)

Plate 3
Detail of a sample mounted in an album
Stripes and checks
Plain weave silk
Akita province; early 20th century
T.172-1963
Sample: 12 x 9 cm ($4^{3}/_{4}$ x $3^{1}/_{2}$ in)
Album: 41.5 x 21.5 cm ($16^{3}/_{8}$ x $8^{1}/_{2}$ in)
Leach Gift

Plate 4
Detail of a *kimono* lining
Rippling water and scattered flowers
Monochrome figured twill silk (*mon aya*) and crêpe silk (*chirimen*) with embroidery in metallic thread
19th century
T.78-1927
176 x 121.5 cm ($69^{1}/_{4}$ x $47^{7}/_{8}$ in)
Clark-Thornhill Gift

Plate 5
Detail of a length
Flowers and lattice (*sayagata*)
Monochrome figured satin silk (*rinzu*)
Mid-19th century
333a-1865
115.5 x 52.5 cm ($45^{1}/_{2}$ x $20^{5}/_{8}$ in)
Queen Victoria Gift

Plate 6
Detail of a length
Bamboo and ivy
Monochrome figured satin silk (*rinzu*)
Mid-19th century
330-1865
965 x 52 cm (380 x $20^{1}/_{2}$ in)
Queen Victoria Gift

Plate 7
Detail of the lining of a Buddhist priest's mantle (*kesa*)
Peonies and scrolling leaves
Figured satin silk
19th century
T.86-1927
105 x 211 cm ($41^{3}/_{8}$ x 83 in)
Clark-Thornhill Gift

Plate 8
Detail of a pair of court trousers (*nagabakama*)
Floral roundel
Figured twill silk
19th century
T.68-1915
128.5 x 32.5 cm ($50^{1}/_{2}$ x $12^{3}/_{4}$ in)
Clark-Thornhill Gift

Plate 9
Detail of a court robe (*kariginu*)
Floral roundel
Figured twill silk
Late 19th century
FE.158-1983
149 x 195 cm ($58^{5}/_{8}$ x $76^{3}/_{4}$ in)

PLATE 10
Detail of a court robe (*kariginu*)
Phoenix and floral roundel
Figured gauze silk
Late 19th century
FE.157-1983
146.5 x 190 cm (57⁵/₈ x 74³/₄ in)

PLATE 11
Detail of a sample
Scrolling paulownia sprays
Figured silk
19th century
1407-1899
36.5 x 41.5 cm (14³/₈ x 16³/₈ in)
Formerly in the Forrer Collection

PLATE 12
Detail of a length
Chrysanthemums
Polychrome figured silk
Mid-19th century
83a-1884
137.5 x 68 cm (54¹/₈ x 26³/₄ in)

PLATE 13
Detail of a sample
Scrolling paulownia, hollyhocks and tiny dragons
Polychrome figured silk
Early to mid-19th century
784.85-1884
30.5 x 31 cm (12 x 12¹/₄ in)

PLATE 14
Detail of the cover of a textile sample book
Deer, crayfish, dragons, fish, crab, coral and phoenixes (*hōō*)
Gold figured silk
Mid-19th century
T.63-1948
29.5 x 40 cm (11⁵/₈ x 15³/₄ in)
Crewdson Gift

PLATE 15
Detail of a sample
Bands of dragons and phoenixes (*hōō*) and floral motifs
Polychrome figured silk
Mid-19th century
784.2-1884
20.5 x 37.5 cm (8 x 14³/₄ in)

PLATE 16
Detail of a sample
Irises
Polychrome figured silk
19th century
751-1905
21 x 13 cm (8¹/₄ x 5¹/₈ in)
Vacher Gift

PLATE 17
Detail of a *kimono*
Flowering plum
Polychrome figured silk
Late 19th century
T.78-1927
167 x 121.5 cm (65³/₄ x 47⁷/₈ in)
Clark-Thornhill Gift

PLATE 18
Detail of a *kimono*
Carp leaping over waves, their tails in the shape of lucky
sceptre-heads encircled in flames
Polychrome figured silk
Late 19th century
T.65-1915
143 x 134 cm (56¹/₄ x 52³/₄ in)
Clark-Thornhill Gift

The image of carp derives from a Chinese story in which any fish
able to leap the waterfall was transformed into a dragon. The story
is a metaphor for achievement and success. (See also plates 20, 53
and 84.) This *kimono* may have belonged to the *kabuki* actor
Ichikawa Danjurō IX.

PLATE 19
Detail of an *obi*
Roundels on a lozenge ground
Polychrome figured silk
19th century
T.85-1927
450 x 33.5 cm (177^1/$_8$ x 13^1/$_8$ in)
Clark-Thornhill Gift

PLATE 20
Detail of a length of *obi* fabric
Carp and cascading water
Polychrome figured silk
Late 19th century
T.208-1934
427 x 69.5 cm (168^1/$_8$ x 27^3/$_8$ in)
Clark-Thornhill Gift

PLATE 21
Detail of a length of *obi* fabric
Cloud-shaped panels with floral motifs on a ground of hexagons
with geometric motifs
Polychrome figured silk
Early 20th century
T.332-1970
407 x 71 cm (160^1/$_4$ x 28 in)

PLATE 22
Detail of a thigh protector (*haidate*) from a suit of armour
Dragons
Polychrome figured silk, silk cord, stencilled leather with iron
chain mail and plates
Last half of 18th century
M.52.5-1909
60 x 55.5 cm (23^5/$_8$ x 21^7/$_8$ in)

PLATE 23
Detail from a sleeve (*kote*), possibly for mounted archery
Floral scrolls and character reading 'yoshi'
Monochrome figured satin silk (*rinzu*), polychrome figured silk,
silk cord, embroidery in metallic thread and iron chain mail
Early 18th century
M.36a-1932
79.5 x 24 cm (31^1/$_4$ x 9^1/$_2$ in)

PLATE 24
Detail of a surcoat (*jimbaori*)
Floral sprays; dragons and clouds
Polychrome figured silk with peacock feathers
18th century
628-1905
83.5 x 133 cm (32^7/$_8$ x 52^3/$_8$ in)
Clark-Thornhill Gift

PLATE 25
Nō robe (*kariginu*)
Chrysanthemums, hexagons and three-comma motifs
Gold figured silk (*kinran*)
Late 18th or early 19th century
FE.8-1984
124 x 140.5 cm (48^3/$_4$ x 55^3/$_8$ in)

PLATE 26
Detail of a *Nō* robe (*atsuita*)
Scrolling clouds
Gold figured silk (*kinran*)
Late 19th century
T.49-1915
147 x 135.5 cm (57^7/$_8$ x 53^3/$_8$ in)
Given by John Hay in memory of his brother Captain GW Hay

PLATE 27
Detail of a *Nō* robe (*karaori*)
Roundels of chrysanthemums, irises and peonies on a lattice
ground
Polychrome figured silk
18th century
T.194-1959
151 x 141 cm (59^1/$_2$ x 55^1/$_2$ in)

PLATE 28
Detail of a panel made from a *Nō* robe (*karaori*)
Pine shoots, chrysanthemums, bush clover and bellflowers
Polychrome banded and figured silk
18th century
T.46-1955
140.5 x 138 cm (55^3/$_8$ x 54^3/$_8$ in)
Alexander Gift

PLATE 29
Detail of a Nō robe (*atsuita*)
Dragon and clouds on a triangle ground
Polychrome figured silk
Mid-18th to mid-19th century
T.297-1963
146 x 132.5 cm (57¹/₂ x 52¹/₈ in)
Edmund de Rothschild Gift

The dragon is the most powerful of the mythical beasts and is an appropriate motif for a robe worn for a male role. (See also plates 22, 24, 125, 138 and 140.)

PLATE 30
Detail of a length, possibly for a theatrical costume
Phoenixes (*hōō*), peonies and scrolling leaves
Polychrome figured open-work silk
Mid-19th century
319a-1865
100 x 64 cm (39³/₈ x 25¹/₄ in)
Queen Victoria Gift

The phoenix, or *hōō*, is an auspicious mythical bird.

PLATE 31
Detail of jacket (*hitatare*), possibly for *Kyōgen*
Floral roundels on a checkerboard ground
Polychrome figured silk
Late 18th or early 19th century
FE.69-1984
89.5 x 167 cm (35¹/₄ x 65³/₄ in)

PLATE 32
Buddhist priest's mantle (*kesa*)
Crests (*mon*) on a lozenge ground with additional patches with floral motif
Polychrome figured silk
19th century
T.140-1927
112.5 x 205 cm (44¹/₄ x 80³/₄ in)
Clark-Thornhill Gift

PLATE 33
Detail of a Buddhist priest's mantle (*kesa*)
Leaf roundels and flower scrolls with additional patches with floral motif
Polychrome figured silk
19th century
T.84-1927
117 x 272 cm (46 x 107 in)
Clark-Thornhill Gift

PLATE 34
Detail of a Buddhist priest's mantle (*kesa*)
Grape vines
Polychrome figured gauze silk
19th century
T.86-1927
105 x 211 cm (41³/₈ x 83 in)
Clark-Thornhill Gift

PLATE 35
Detail of a Buddhist priest's mantle (*kesa*)
Butterflies and peonies with additional patches with mock Sanskrit letters and silk cord
Polychrome figured banded silk
19th century
T.80-1927
114.5 x 201.5 cm (45 x 79³/₈ in)
Clark-Thornhill Gift

PLATE 36
Detail of a Buddhist textile
Roundels of gentian leaves and bamboo, pine shoots and stylised bamboo stripes against a lattice ground
Polychrome figured silk
19th century
T.92-1927
100 x 100 cm (39³/₈ x 39³/₈ in) on diagonal
Clark-Thornhill Gift

On the reverse, in black ink, there is a dedicatory inscription.

PLATE 37
Detail of a Buddhist textile
Bunches of camellia, bellflowers and grasses on a checked
matt ground
Polychrome figured silk
About 1873
T.93-1927
86.5 x 147 cm (34 x 57⁷/₈ in)
Clark-Thornhill Gift

On the reverse, in black ink, there is a inscription dedicating this
textile to the Shonen-ji temple on the seventh month of Meiji six
(= July 1873).

PLATE 38
Detail of a Buddhist textile
Roundels of chrysanthemums and scrolling paulownia
Polychrome figured silk
19th century
Circ.157-1927
92 x 65 cm (36¹/₄ x 25¹/₂ in) triangular
Clark-Thornhill Gift

PLATE 39
Detail of a Buddhist textile
Peonies
Polychrome figured silk
Late 19th century
T.88-1927
67 x 66.5 cm (26³/₈ x 26¹/₈ in)
Clark-Thornhill Gift

PLATE 40
Detail of a hanging from a Buddhist temple
Sakyamuni; the historical Buddha
Silk woven with human hair
Late 18th or 19th century
T.98-1927
Whole: 119.5 x 51.5 cm (47 x 20¹/₄ in)
Image: 100.5 x 42.5 cm (39¹/₂ x 16³/₄ in)
Clark-Thornhill Gift

According to information received with this object, in the Meiwa
era (1764–71) there was a deluge in the village of Takawaka, in
Etchu province. Those that survived the flood believed they had
been saved by Sakyamuni, so in thanks they wove this hanging and
presented it to the local temple.

PLATE 41
Detail of a hanging
Irises by a stream
Tapestry weave silk (*tsuzuri-ori*)
19th century
T.161-1969
201 x 137 cm (79¹/₈ x 54 in)
Curlender Gift

PLATE 42
Detail of a gift cover (*fukusa*)
Cranes
Tapestry weave silk (*tsuzuri-ori*)
Late 19th century
T.262-1959
72.5 x 65 cm (28¹/₂ x 25¹/₂ in)

Cranes symbolise longevity as they are believed to live for a
thousand years. (See also plates 75, 78, 101 and 132.) This textile
has a label from the Echigo-ya, the most famous drapery store in
the Edo and Meiji periods.

PLATE 43
Detail of a sample mounted in an album
Stripes and arrows
Velvet (*birōdo*) woven with selectively pre-dyed yarns
Late 19th century
T.177-1953
Sample: 13 x 7 cm (5¹/₈ x 2³/₄ in)
Album: 23 x 34.5 cm (9 x 13¹/₂ in)

PLATE 44
Detail of a gift cover (*fukusa*)
Five Fowls
Tapestry velvet (*tsuzure birōdo*)
Mid-19th century
361-1880
80 x 72 cm (31¹/₂ x 28³/₈ in)

The woven seals on the left of this gift cover suggest that this design was derived from a work by the painter Maruyama Ōkyo (1733–95). The cock, hen and three chicks symbolise a family living in harmony.

PLATE 45
Hanging scroll
Birds on a fruiting bough above rocks and peonies
Painted, ribbed and cut velvet (*birōdo-yūzen*)
About 1878–88
1712-1888
Scroll: 195 x 73.5 cm (76³/₄ x 29 in)
Image: 127.5 x 59 cm (50¹/₈ x 23¹/₄ in)

PLATE 46
Detail of a hanging scroll
Parrot and fruiting bough
Painted, ribbed and cut velvet (*birōdo-yūzen*)
About 1878–88
1709-1888
Scroll: 194 x 73.5 cm (76³/₈ x 29 in)
Image: 128.5 x 58.5 cm (50¹/₂ x 23 in)

PLATE 47
Picture
The Yomei-mon gate of the Tōshōgū shrine at Nikkō
Painted, ribbed and cut velvet (*birōdo-yūzen*)
Late 19th or early 20th century
T.104-1971
66.5 x 61 cm (26¹/₈ x 24 in)

The shrine at Nikkō is dedicated to Tokugawa Ieyasu (1542–1616).

PLATE 48
Detail of a length
Checks, streams and step pattern
Plain weave cotton woven with selectively pre-dyed yarns (*kasuri*)
Ryūkyū Islands; 19th century
T.110-1957
50 x 33 cm (19⁵/₈ x 13 in)

PLATE 49
Detail of a sample mounted in an album
Checks, streams and step pattern
Plain weave cotton woven with selectively pre-dyed yarns (*kasuri*)
Ryūkyū Islands; 19th century
T.142-1968
Sample: 18.5 x 23 cm (7¹/₄ x 9 in)
Album: 27 x 41 cm (10⁵/₈ x 16¹/₈ in)

PLATE 50
Detail of a bedding cover (*futon-ji*)
Concentric squares and diagonally connected squares
Plain weave cotton woven with selectively pre-dyed yarns (*kasuri*)
Katanose, Ukiha-gun; late 19th century
T.326-1960
200 x 93.5 cm (78³/₄ x 36⁷/₈ in)

PLATE 51
Detail of a bedding cover (*futon-ji*)
Pine tree, crane and tortoise alternating with diagonally paired squares
Plain weave cotton woven with selectively pre-dyed yarns (*kasuri*)
Chikugogawa district; Fukuoka prefecture; late 19th century
T.98-1969
174 x 160 cm (68¹/₂ x 63 in)

The pine, crane and tortoise are all symbols of longevity.

PLATE 52
Sample
Shishi and peonies
Plain weave cotton woven with selectively pre-dyed yarns (*kasuri*)
Late 19th century
T.126-1968
37 x 31 cm (14¹/₂ x 12¹/₄ in)

A *shishi* is a mythical beast, rather like a lion. It is often shown dancing among peonies to celebrate long life and happiness. (See also plate 128.)

PLATE 53
Detail of a length
Carp
Plain weave bast fibre (*asa*) woven with selectively pre-dyed yarns (*kasuri*)
Kurume; 19th century
T.99-1957
140 x 33 cm (55¹/₈ x 13 in)

PLATE 54
Detail of a *kimono*
Chrysanthemums and hatched design
Plain weave bast fibre (*asa*) woven with selectively pre-dyed yarns (*kasuri*)
Ojiya (Niigata prefecture); 19th century
T.329-1960
133.5 x 122.5 cm (52¹/₂ x 48¹/₄ in)

Niigata prefecture, or Echigo as the area was known in the Edo period, was famous for its fine *kasuri* cloth.

PLATE 55
Detail of a *kimono* for a child
Stripes
Plain weave silk woven with selectively pre-dyed yarns (*kasuri*)
Late 19th century
FE.51-1982
93.5 x 85 cm (36⁷/₈ x 33¹/₂ in)

PLATE 56
Detail of a length
Stripes
Open-work plain weave silk
About 1874
AP.43.3-1876
1166 x 56 cm (459 x 22 in)

This length was exhibited at the London Exhibition of 1874.

PLATE 57
Detail of a length
Stripes
Open-work plain weave silk
About 1874
AP.43.6-1876
156 x 42.5 cm (61³/₈ x 16³/₄ in)

This length was exhibited at the London Exhibition of 1874.

PLATE 58
Page from a sample book
Plain weave silk, woven to produce a puckered effect
Late 19th century
T.55-1957
Sample: 14.5 x 16 cm (5³/₄ x 6¹/₄ in)
Album: 24 x 33 cm (9¹/₂ x 13 in)

PLATE 59
Detail of a coat (*michiyuki*)
Flowers against a lattice and spot ground
Figured crêpe artificial silk
About 1920–30
FE.23-1989
116 x 123.5 cm (45⁵/₈ x 48⁵/₈ in)

PLATE 60
Detail of a *kimono*
Lilies against a diagonally striped ground
Plain weave silk woven with yarns selectively pre-dyed using stencils
Probably Kanto district; about 1930–50
FE.162-1988
139.5 x 124.5 cm (55 x 49 in)

PLATE 61
Detail of a *kimono* entitled *Ise*
By Shimura Fukumi (b.1924)
Checks
Plain weave silk
Kyoto; 1988
FE.11-1989
167.5 x 138 cm (66 x 54³/₈ in)

The title of this *kimono* comes from the tenth-century *Tales of Ise*. This famous work of literature was an important subject for artists and designers of the Rimpa school. The colour scheme of this *kimono* was inspired by the rich palette of Rimpa painting.

PLATE 62
Detail of a coat (*michiyuki*)
By Kitamura Takeshi (b.1935)
Lozenges
Gauze weave silk
Kyoto; 1993 (made up 1994–5)
FE.274-1995
135 x 132 cm (53¹/₈ x 52 in)

PLATE 63
Detail of *Puffed Blocks*
By Arai Jun'ichi (b.1932)
Checks
Plain weave cotton and polyester
Tokyo; 1979
T.148-1990
322 x 60 cm (126³/₄ x 23⁵/₈ in)

PLATE 64
Detail of *Seaweed Scarf*
By Miyamoto Eiji (b.1948)
Stripes
Triple weave silk, polyamide and polyurethane
1992
FE.282-1995
195 x 32 cm (76³/₄ x 12¹/₂ in)

PLATE 65
Detail of a *kimono* fragment
Cascading cherry blossoms and chains, notched lozenges and circular motifs on a hazy gold ground
Monochrome figured satin silk (*rinzu*) with applied gold leaf (*surihaku*), tie-dyeing *(kanoko shibori)* and embroidery in silk and metallic thread
First half of 17ᵗʰ century
1588-1899
58.5 x 30 cm (23 x 11⁷/₈ in)
Formerly in the Forrer Collection

PLATE 66
Detail of a *kimono*
Peonies on a fretwork ground
Crêpe silk (*chirimen*) with tie-dyeing (*kanoko shibori*), paste-resist dyeing (*yūzen*) and embroidery in silk and metallic threads
First half of 19ᵗʰ century
T.109-1954
155 x 124 cm (61 x 48⁷/₈ in)
Hart Gift

PLATE 67
Detail of a *kimono*
Roundels of pine, bamboo and plum on a hemp leaf ground
Monochrome figured satin silk (*rinzu*) with tie-dyeing (*kanoko shibori*)
First half of 19ᵗʰ century
FE.32-1982
150 x 123.5 cm (59 x 48⁵/₈ in)

The pine, bamboo and plum are three of the most popular natural motifs. They are symbols of longevity, perseverance and renewal and are often shown in combination with one another. (See also plates 83 and 110.)

PLATE 68
Kimono
Plum blossoms and paper gift ornaments in the shape
of butterflies
Monochrome figured satin silk (*rinzu*) with tie-dyeing (*kanoko
shibori*) and embroidery in silk and metallic thread
First half of 19th century
FE.28-1984
179 x 124 cm (70^1/$_2$ x 48^7/$_8$ in)

PLATE 69
Detail of a *kimono*
Plum blossoms, bamboo and clouds
Crêpe silk (*chirimen*) with bound (*kanoko shibori*) and stitched tie-
dying (*nuishime shibori*), the latter areas scored with gold, and
embroidery in silk and metallic thread
About 1912–30
FE.17-1994
168 x 128 cm (66^1/$_8$ x 50^3/$_8$ in)

PLATE 70
Detail of a *kimono*
Hexagons with floral centres, chrysanthemums and plum blossom
Monochrome figured satin silk (*rinzu*) with stencilled imitation tie-
dyeing (*kata kanoko*) and embroidery in silk and metallic thread
Mid-18th century
FE.13-1983
163 x 127 cm (64^1/$_8$ x 50 in)

PLATE 71
Detail of a *kimono*
Hollyhocks, paulownia and snowflakes
Monochrome figured satin silk (*rinzu*) with stencilled imitation
tie-dying (*kata kanoko*), brushed pigments and embroidery in silk
and metallic threads
Late 18th or early 19th century
FE.8-1987
161 x 122 cm (63^3/$_8$ x 48 in)

PLATE 72
Detail of a *kimono*
Bamboo and characters
Monochrome figured satin silk (*rinzu*) with stencilled imitation
tie-dying *(kata kanoko)*, brushed pigments and embroidery in silk
and metallic thread
Late 18th century
FE.106-1982
156 x 123.5 cm (61^3/$_8$ x 48^5/$_8$ in)

The characters come from poems in the *Kokinshū* anthology,
compiled about AD 905.

PLATE 73
Detail of the pleated shoulder of a *samurai* jacket (*kataginu*)
Curved arrangement of small dots known as *same* (sharkskin)
with crest (*mon*)
Plain weave bast fibre (*asa*) with small-scale stencilling (*komon*),
stencilling (*katazome*) and brushed pigments
19th century
FE.46-1980
68 x 75 cm (26^3/$_4$ x 29^1/$_2$ in)

PLATE 74
Page of a sample book
Small dots and floral motifs
Plain weave cotton with small-scale stencilling (*komon*)
Book dated 1850
T.150-1959
Samples: 6.2 x 5 cm (2^1/$_2$ x 2 in)
Book: 19.5 x 28 cm (7^5/$_8$ x 11 in)

PLATE 75
Detail of a bedding cover (*futon-ji*)
Cranes and pine trees in the snow
Plain weave cotton with stencilled decoration (*katazome*)
Late 19th century
FE.113-1997
150 x 122 cm (59 x 48 in)

PLATE 76
Detail of a fisherman's celebratory robe (*maiwai*)
Ebisu in a treasure ship
Plain weave cotton with stencilled decoration (*katazome*)
Early 20th century
FE.102-1982
136 x 131 cm (53^1/$_2$ x 51^1/$_2$ in)

Ebisu is one of the Seven Gods of Good Luck.

PLATE 77
Detail of a sleeping coverlet (*yogi*)
Floral checks
Plain weave cotton with printed and stencilled decoration (*sarasa*)
Sakai; 19th century
FE.155-1983
190 x 176 cm (74^7/$_8$ x 69^1/$_4$ in)

PLATE 78
Detail of a robe
Crane, pine trees and clouds
Plain weave cotton with stencilled decoration (*bingata*)
Shuri, Okinawa, Ryūkyū Islands; 19th century
T.18-1963
132 x 128 cm (52 x 50^3/$_8$ in)

PLATE 79
Detail of a robe
Maple leaves
Plain weave cotton with stencilled decoration (*bingata*)
Shuri, Okinawa, Ryūkyū Islands; 19th century
T.295-1960
126 x 124 cm (49^5/$_8$ x 48^7/$_8$ in)

PLATE 80
Detail of a robe
Staggered lozenges
Plain weave banana fibre (*bashō*) with indigo-dyed stencilled
decoration (*aigata*)
Ryūkyū Islands; late 19th or early 20th century
FE.7-1983
147 x 116.5 cm (57^7/$_8$ x 45^7/$_8$ in)

PLATE 81
Detail of a length
Tortoise
Plain weave cotton with paste-resist decoration (*tsutsugaki*)
Late 19th century
T.134-1968
138.5 x 31 cm (54^1/$_2$ x 12^1/$_4$ in)

The tortoise is a symbol of longevity.

PLATE 82
Detail of a length mounted on a scroll
Umbrella, tree and acorns
Plain weave cotton with paste-resist decoration (*tsutsugaki*)
Late 19th century
T.216-1964
Scroll: 104 x 32 cm (40^7/$_8$ x 12^1/$_2$ in)
Image: 44.5 x 27 cm (17^1/$_2$ x 10^5/$_8$ in)

PLATE 83
Bedding cover (*futon-ji*), adapted from a sleeping coverlet (*yogi*)
Plum blossom with pine and bamboo, with crest
Plain weave cotton with paste-resist decoration (*tsutsugaki*)
Late 19th century
T.332-1960
147 x 143 cm (57^7/$_8$ x 56^1/$_4$ in)

PLATE 84
Detail of a bedding cover (*futon-ji*)
Fish roundel
Plain weave cotton with paste-resist decoration (*tsutsugaki*)
Late 19th century
T.199-1964
218 x 151 cm (85^7/$_8$ x 59^1/$_2$ in)

PLATE 85
Detail of a festival banner, used as the backing of a temple hanging
Samurai warrior
Plain weave cotton with paste-resist decoration (*tsutsugaki*)
19th century
T.132-1927
270 x 178 cm (106^1/$_4$ x 70 in)
Hadden Gift

PLATE 86
Detail of a doorway curtain (*noren*)
Octopus
Plain weave cotton with paste-resist decoration (*tsutsugaki*)
Early 20th century
FE.49-1982
95.5 x 63 cm (37¹/₂ x 24³/₄ in)

PLATE 87
Detail of a length
River and fish beside shore with chrysanthemums and plum
blossoms
Plain weave bast fibre (*asa*) with paste-resist decoration (*tsutsugaki*)
Late 19th century
T.136-1968
73 x 35 cm (28³/₄ x 13³/₄ in)

PLATE 88
Detail of a length
Cascading wisteria
Plain weave bast fibre (*asa*) with paste-resist decoration (*yūzen*)
Mid-19th century
T.137-1968
124.5 x 32 cm (49 x 12¹/₂ in)

PLATE 89
Detail of a summer *kimono* (*katabira*)
Chrysanthemums, clouds and butterflies
Plain weave bast-fibre (*asa*) with paste-resist decoration (*yūzen*) and
tie-dyeing (*kanoko shibori*)
19th century
T.17-1963
126 x 114 cm (49⁵/₈ x 44⁷/₈ in)

PLATE 90
Sample mounted in an album
Squirrel on a grape vine
Gauze silk with paste-resist decoration (*yūzen*)
19th century
T.50-1935
Sample: 24 x 18 cm (9¹/₂ x 7 in)
Album: 29.5 x 42.5 cm (11⁵/₈ x 16³/₄ in)
Gilbertson Gift

PLATE 91
Sample mounted in an album
Ox-cart wheels and maple leaves
Plain weave silk with paste-resist decoration (*yūzen*)
19th century
T.175-1953
Sample: 30 x 17 cm (11⁷/₈ x 6⁵/₈ in)
Album: 35.5 x 24 cm (14 x 9¹/₂ in)

PLATE 92
Sample mounted in an album
Scrolling paulownia
Plain weave silk with paste-resist decoration (*yūzen*) and
embroidery in silk and metallic thread
Late 19th century
T.49-1935
Sample: 24.5 x 34.5 cm (9⁵/₈ x 13¹/₂ in)
Album: 30.5 x 40.5 cm (12 x 16 in)
Gilbertson Gift

PLATE 93
Detail of a *kimono* section
Peonies
Monochrome figured satin silk (*rinzu*) with paste-resist decoration
(*yūzen*), stencilled imitation tie-dyeing (*kata kanoko*) and
embroidery in silk and metallic threads
Mid-19th century
79-1884
164 x 166.5 cm (64¹/₂ x 65¹/₂ in)

PLATE 94
Detail of a *kimono*
Rippling water, bamboo and birds
Monochrome figured satin silk (*rinzu*) with paste-resist decoration
(*yūzen*) and embroidery in silk and metallic thread
Late 19th century
874-1891
160 x 125.5 cm (63 x 49³/₈ in)

The Museum bought this *kimono* in 1891 from Liberty's in Regent
Street, London.

PLATE 95
Detail of a *kimono*
Pine trees and clouds
Crêpe silk (*chirimen*) with paste-resist decoration (*yūzen*), areas of
scored gold and touches of embroidery in silk thread
First half of 19th century
T.266-1968
155 x 124 cm (61 x 48⁷/₈ in)
Given by Lady Palairet in memory of Sir Michael Palairet

This *kimono* once belonged to the great Japanese textile collector
and dealer Nomura Shōjirō.

PLATE 96
Detail of a *kimono*
Tortoise, pine trees, waves and a lacquer box
Crêpe silk (*chirimen*) with paste-resist dyeing (*yūzen*), stencilled
imitation tie-dying (*kata kanoko*) and embroidery in silk and
metallic thread
Late 19th or early 20th century
T.155-1965
165 x 122 cm (65 x 48 in)
Leach Gift

The motifs on this *kimono* illustrate the tale of Urashima Taro.
Urashima was a fisherman who one day mistakenly caught a
tortoise, which he kindly returned to the sea. The following day he
saw a beautiful woman clinging to a wreck. He rescued her and
helped her return to her home. The woman was Otomine, one of
the princesses in the court of the Dragon King of the Sea. Otomine
and Urashima were married and lived for three happy years in the
Dragon King's realm until the fisherman began to get homesick.
Otomine begged him not to go and revealed that she had been the
tortoise he had saved. Urashima would not be dissuaded, however,
and left taking with him a treasure box given by Otomine with the
strict instructions that if he wanted to ever see her again he must
not open the box. Returning to his home, Urashima was puzzled to
discover that his family had died out. On finding his own tomb he
was so distraught that, forgetting Otomine's instructions, he
opened the box hoping to find an explanation. He discovered that
in the three years he had lived with his wife, three hundred years
had passed in the real world. He was now a very old man and his
spirit left him, dead, on his own tomb.

PLATE 97
Detail of a length
Bamboo and blossoming trees
Crêpe silk (*chirimen*) with resist-dyed decoration (*yūzen*)
About 1865–7
842-1869
1800 x 40 cm (708⁵/₈ x 15³/₄ in)

This length was exhibited at the Paris International Exhibition of
1867.

PLATE 98
Detail of a *kimono*
Lengths of fabric on a stand with clouds and cherry blossoms
Crêpe silk (*chirimen*) with paste-resist decoration (*yūzen*) and
embroidery in silk and metallic thread
Late 19th century
FE.29-1987
169 x 129 cm (66¹/₂ x 50³/₄ in)

PLATE 99
Gift cover (*fukusa*)
Gosekku motifs
Plain weave silk with paste-resist decoration (*yūzen*) and
embroidery in metallic thread
Late 19th century
T.260-1959
75.5 x 69.5 cm (29³/₄ x 27³/₈ in)

The motifs on this gift cover represent the *Gosekku*, the five
seasonal festivals. The lobsters indicate New Year (see plate 135),
the peach blossoms the festival held on 3 March, the iris and
mugwort that of 5 May, the *kemeri* ball – use in a court game – and
the paper mulberry leaves that of 7 July and the chrysanthemums
that of 9 September. The ribbon-like bundle is a *noshi*, an
ornament originally made from strips of dried abalone which is
traditionally tied to goodwill gifts.

PLATE 100
Detail of a length
Chrysanthemums and camellias against a bamboo fence
Crêpe silk (*chirimen*) with paste-resist decoration (*yūzen*)
Early 20th century
T.429-1912
86 x 41 cm (33⁷/₈ x 16¹/₈ in)
Strange Gift

PLATE 101
Detail of a *kimono*
Cranes flying above a river, mountains and cherry blossoms
Crêpe silk (*chirimen*) with paste-resist decoration (*yūzen*) and
touches of embroidery in silk thread
Early 20th century
FE.233-1974
160 x 124 cm (63 x 48⁷/₈ in)
Hardcastle Gift

PLATE 102
Detail of a *kimono*
Chrysanthemums, cherry blossoms, clouds and haze
Crêpe silk (*chirimen*) with paste-resist decoration (*chaya-zome*),
stencilled imitation tie-dyeing (*kata kanoko*) and embroidery in silk
and metallic thread
First half of 19th century
FE.12-1983
141 x 125 cm (55¹/₂ x 49¹/₄ in)

PLATE 103
Detail of a summer *kimono* (*katabira*)
Irises by a bridge
Plain weave bast fibre (*asa*) with paste-resist decoration (*chaya-zome*), stencilled imitation tie-dyeing (*kata kanoko*) and embroidery
in silk and metallic thread
First half of 19th century
T.87-1968
175 x 122 cm (68⁷/₈ x 48 in)
G Saumarez Gift

The iris and bridge motif relates to a famous passage in the tenth-century *Tales of Ise*, one of the most famous works of classical
Japanese literature. In the ninth chapter the hero Ariwara no
Narihira comes to a place in Mikawa Province noted for its
eightfold bridge and irises and composes a poem using the
syllables of *kakitsubata*, the Japanese word for iris, as the first
syllable of each of the lines.

PLATE 104
Detail of a jacket (*haori*)
Flowers and triangular motifs
Figured crêpe silk with printed decoration
About 1920–30
FE.163-1988
92.5 x 125 cm (36³/₈ x 49¹/₄ in)

PLATE 105
Detail of a *kimono*
Paulownia and clouds
Monochrome figured satin silk (*rinzu*) with paste-resist
decoration (*yūzen*), embroidery in silk and metallic thread and
applied gold leaf
About 1930–50
FE.67-1997
151 x 129 cm (59¹/₂ x 50³/₄ in)
Navaro Gift

PLATE 106
Page from sample book
Landscape at Ishiyama-dera, a Buddhist temple near Lake Biwa
Crêpe silk or artificial silk (*chirimen*) with paste-resist decoration
(*yūzen*)
Book dated 1937
FE.21-1997
Sample: 31 x 36 cm (12¹/₄ x 14¹/₈ in) when folded out
Book: 24.5 x 47 cm (9⁵/₈ x 18¹/₂ in)

PLATE 107
Page from sample book
Bamboo
Monochrome figured satin silk or artificial silk (*rinzu*) with printed decoration
Book dated 1938
FE.18-1997
Sample: 13.5 x 35 cm (5³/₈ x 13³/₄ in)
Book: 34 x 43.5 cm (13³/₈ x 17¹/₈ in)

PLATE 108
Page from sample book
Poppies
Crêpe silk or artificial silk (*chirimen*) with printed decoration
Book dated 1938
FE.18-1997
Sample: 27 x 35 cm (10⁵/₈ x 13³/₄ in)
Book: 34 x 43.5 cm (13³/₈ x 17¹/₈ in)

PLATE 109
Page from sample book
Butterflies and peonies
Figured crêpe silk or artificial silk (*chirimen*) with printed decoration
Book dated 1939
FE.22-1997
Sample: 36 x 35.5 cm (14¹/₈ x 14 in) when folded out
Album: 24.5 x 47.5 cm (9⁵/₈ x 18³/₄ in)

PLATE 110
Detail of an underkimono (*juban*)
Bamboo, plum and clouds
Figured twill silk with printed decoration
About 1940–50
FE.14-1987
126 x 119 cm (49⁵/₈ x 46⁷/₈ in)

PLATE 111
Detail of an underkimono (*juban*)
Wide diagonal stripes
Plain weave silk with tie-dyeing (*shibori*)
About 1940–50
FE.15-1987
150 x 123 cm (59 x 48³/₈ in)

PLATE 112
Detail of a jacket (*haori*)
Roses
Crêpe silk (*chirimen*) with paste-resist (*yūzen*) and hand-painted decoration
About 1950–60
FE.128-1988
87 x 127 cm (34¹/₄ x 50 in)

PLATE 113
Detail of a *kimono*
Fans, flowers and flowing water
Monochrome figured satin silk or artificial silk (*rinzu*) with printed decoration
About 1965–75
FE.127-1988
142 x 123 cm (56 x 48³/₈ in)

PLATE 114
Page from sample book
Flowers and small dots
Plain weave artificial silk with printed decoration
Book dated 1966–9
FE.25-1997
Samples: approximately 32 x 4 cm (12¹/₂ x 1¹/₂ in)
Book: 38.5 x 54.5 cm (15¹/₈ x 21¹/₂ in)

PLATE 115
Page from sample book
Umbrellas
Figured artificial silk with printed decoration
Book dated 1978
FE.23-1997
Sample: 8 x 20 cm (3¹/₈ x 7⁷/₈ in)
Book: 35.5 x 27.5 cm (14 x 10⁷/₈ in)

PLATE 116
Detail of a screen showing the stages of paper making
By Serizawa Keisuke (1895–1984)
Drying sheets of paper in the sun
Plain weave silk with stencilled decoration (*bingata*)
About 1938
FE.20-1985
81.5 x 214 cm (32 x 84¹/₄ in)

PLATE 117
Detail of a *kimono* entitled *Myriad Green Leaves*
By Furusawa Machiko (b.1933)
Dragonflies, flowers and clouds
Figured silk with tie-dyeing (*shibori*) and hand-painted decoration
Ōita prefecture; 1992
FE.422-1992
161 x 121 cm (63³/₈ x 47⁵/₈ in)

PLATE 118
Detail of a *kimono* entitled *Green Waves*
By Moriguchi Kunihiko (b.1941)
Abstract wave pattern
Plain weave silk with paste-resist decoration (*yūzen*)
Kyoto; 1973
FE.420-1992
158 x 129.5 cm (62¹/₄ x 51 in)

PLATE 119
Detail of a *kimono* entitled *Flight*
By Matsubara Yoshichi (b.1937)
Abstract pattern
Crêpe silk (*chirimen*) with stencilled decoration (*katazome*)
Tokyo; 1990
FE.10-1995
169 x 131 cm (66¹/₂ x 51¹/₂ in)

PLATE 120
Detail of a *kimono*
Chrysanthemums against a fence
Monochrome figured satin silk (*rinzu*) with embroidery in silk and metallic thread
Mid-19th century
T.269-1960
169 x 123 cm 66¹/₂ x 48³/₈ in)
Mockett Gift

PLATE 121
Detail of a *kimono*
Roundels of hollyhocks and paulownia, lilies and pine trees
Satin silk (*shu*) with embroidery in silk and metallic thread
Mid-19th century
FE.11-1983
172 x 124 cm (67³/₄ x 48⁷/₈ in)

PLATE 122
Detail of a *kimono*
Ducks on rippling water
Satin silk (*shu*) with embroidery in silk and metallic thread
Mid-19th century
FE.28-1987
170 x 126 cm (67 x 49⁵/₈ in)

This *kimono* is believed to have been part of a wedding outfit. The paired ducks symbolise marital harmony. (See also plate 123.)

PLATE 123
Detail of a *kimono*
Ducks on rippling water among irises and pinks
Satin silk (*shu*) with embroidery in silk and metallic thread
Mid-19th century
T.79-1927
164 x 121 cm (64¹/₂ x 47⁵/₈ in)
Clark-Thornhill Gift

PLATE 124
Detail of a *kimono*
Mountain top pavilion with waterfall and blossoming tree with broom
Satin silk (*shu*) with embroidery in silk and metallic thread
Mid-19th century
FE.36-1981
175.5 x 126 cm (69 x 49⁵/₈ in)

PLATE 125
Detail of a *kimono*
Dragon and Mount Fuji
Satin silk (*shu*) with embroidery in silk and metallic thread
Late 19th century
T.72-1957
142 x 127 cm (55⁷/₈ x 50 in)
Hughes Gift

PLATE 126
Detail of a *kimono*
Birds, butterflies, wisteria and lilies
Satin silk (*shu*) with embroidery in silk and metallic thread
Late 19th century
T.178-1967
144 x 124 cm (56⁵/₈ x 48⁷/₈ in)

PLATE 127
Detail of an *obi*
Ox-cart wheels, lozenges, wisteria and peonies
Velvet (*birōdo*) with embroidery in silk and metallic thread
First half of 19th century
FE.23-1973
400 x 25.5 cm (157¹/₂ x 10 in)
Douglas Watson Gift

PLATE 128
Detail of an *obi*
Shishi and peonies
Satin silk (*shu*) with embroidery in silk and metallic thread
First half of 19th century
T.270-1960
364 x 25 cm (143¹/₄ x 9⁷/₈ in)
Mockett Gift

PLATE 129
Detail of a gift cover (*fukusa*)
Milk vetch
Satin silk (*shu*) with embroidery in silk and metallic thread
First half of 19th century
Circ.169-1927
77.5 x 73 cm (30¹/₂ x 28³/₄ in)
Clark-Thornhill Gift

The milk vetch is one of the seven plants traditionally gathered at New Year. The plants are made into a soup that is believed to prevent illness.

PLATE 130
Gift cover (*fukusa*)
Washing the white elephant
Satin silk (*shu*) with embroidery in silk and metallic thread
First half of 19th century
T.94-1927
92.5 x 70 cm (36³/₈ x 27¹/₂ in)
Clark-Thornhill Gift

In 1728 two Indian elephants were brought to Nagasaki from China. The design on this *fukusa* implies that the gift it covers is also a great rarity and has been as carefully prepared as one of the elephants was when presented to the *shōgun* in 1729.

PLATE 131
Detail of a gift cover (*fukusa*)
Jo and Uba
Satin silk (*shu*) with embroidery in silk and metallic thread
First half of 19th century
T.236-1967
79.5 x 81 cm (31¹/₄ x 31⁷/₈ in)

Jo and Uba were an old couple who lived a long and happy life together. When they died their spirits occupied the pine trees on the island where they had lived and on moonlit nights they returned to human form to clear the forest floor. Jo raked in the good and Uba swept out the bad.

PLATE 132
Detail of a gift cover (*fukusa*)
Cranes
Satin silk (*shu*) with embroidery in silk and metallic thread
First half of 19th century
T.20-1923
84 x 67 cm (33 x 26³/₈ in)
Watts Gift

PLATE 133
Detail of a gift cover (*fukusa*)
Castle and bridge
Satin silk (*shu*) with embroidery in metallic thread
First half of 19th century
T.47-1910
79.5 x 66.5 cm (31¼ x 26⅛ in)

PLATE 134
Detail of a gift cover (*fukusa*)
The Seven Sages of the Bamboo Grove
Satin silk (*shu*) with embroidery in silk and metallic thread
Mid-19th century
T.197-1963
76 x 70 cm (30 x 27½ in)
Dunlop Gift

The Seven Sages were a group of Chinese Taoist philosophers who gathered in a bamboo grove to talk and drink.

PLATE 135
Gift cover (*fukusa*)
Lobsters
Satin silk (*shu*) with embroidery in silk thread
Mid-19th century
81-1884
75.5 x 69 cm (29¾ x 27⅛ in)

The two lobsters represent Izanagi-no-mikoto and Izanami-no-mikoto, the two gods enshrined at Ise, Japan's most important Shintō shrine. It was traditional to visit Ise in the New Year.

PLATE 136
Hanging from a Buddhist temple
Kannon
Figured silk with embroidery in silk and metallic thread
Late 18th or early 19th century
T.208-1958
159 x 89.5 cm (62½ x 35¼ in)
Allen Gift

PLATE 137
Detail of a Buddhist textile
Roundels with mock Sanskrit characters on lotus flowers against a diapered ground with floral borders
Monochrome figured satin silk (*rinzu*) with embroidery in silk and metallic thread
Late 18th or early 19th century
T.97-1927
215 x 192.5 cm (84⅝ x 75¾ in)
Clark-Thornhill Gift

PLATE 138
Detail of a Buddhist textile
Dragons and clouds
Plain weave cotton with embroidery in silk and metallic thread
19th century
Circ.167-1927
43 x 77 cm (17 x 30⅜ in) triangular
Clark-Thornhill Gift

PLATE 139
Detail of a Buddhist textile
Hexagons of floral and bird motifs
Plain weave cotton with embroidery in silk and metallic thread
19th century
T.96-1927
43 x 76 cm (17 x 30 in) triangular
Clark-Thornhill Gift

PLATE 140
Detail of a hanging from a Buddhist temple, possibly the Daitoku-ji Temple in Kyoto
Dragon
Plain weave cotton with embroidery in silk and metallic thread
19th century
T.132-1927
270 x 178 cm (106¼ x 70 in)
Hadden Gift

PLATE 141
Hanging, possibly from a Buddhist temple
Landscape with peacock and peahen below a curtain of brocade
panels and a flaming drum, phoenixes and dragons
Plain weave cotton with embroidery in silk and metallic threads
19th century
T.252-1921
268 x 213 cm (105^1/$_2$ x 83^7/$_8$ in)

This image alludes to part of *bugaku*, a ritual dance, during which a
drum, or *da-daioka*, is beaten.

PLATE 142
Detail of a hanging from the Chio-in Temple, Kyoto
Eagle carrying away a *shishi* cub with scared monkeys below
Plain weave cotton with embroidery in silk and metallic thread
19th century
167-1898
250 x 164 cm (98^3/$_8$ x 64^1/$_2$ in)

PLATE 143
Detail of a hanging, possibly from a Buddhist temple
Treasure ships, cranes and tortoises
Plain weave cotton with embroidery in silk and metallic thread
Late 19th century
T.94-1958
205 x 133 cm (80^3/$_4$ x 52^3/$_8$ in)
Eley and Warren Gift

The treasure ship conveys a wish for wealth or an abundant
harvest.

PLATE 144
Hanging
Scattered fans
Plain weave cotton with embroidery in silk and metallic thread
Late 19th century
T.200-1968
284 x 278 cm (111^7/$_8$ x 109^1/$_2$ in)
Hutchins Gift

PLATE 145
Hanging
Pine trees on the shore
Plain weave silk embroidery in silk thread
Early 20th century
T.5A-1911
250 x 310 cm (98^1/$_2$ x 122 in)

This large hanging was exhibited at the Japan-Britain Exhibition of
1910.

PLATE 146
Page from a sample book of works by students of Kyoto Prefectural
Girl's School exhibited at the London International Health
Exhibition of 1884
Thistle
Satin silk (*shu*) with embroidery in silk thread
Kyoto; 1884
1080-1884
Sample: 22 x 19 cm (8^5/$_8$ x 7^1/$_2$ in)
Book: 24.5 x 30.5 cm (9^5/$_8$ x 12 in)

This piece of work was executed by 15-year-old Okamoto Michiyo,
a 4th grade embroidery student.

PLATE 147
Detail of a work coat
Lozenges
Plain weave cotton quilted in cotton thread (*sashiko*)
Late 19th century
FE.30-1982
124.5 x 122 cm (49 x 48 in)

PLATE 148
Detail of a *kimono*
Lozenges
Plain weave bast fibre (*asa*) with cotton stitch embroidery (*kogin*)
Tsugaru district (Aomori prefecture); late 19th or early 20th century
FE.141-1983
128 x 102 cm (50^3/$_8$ x 40^1/$_8$ in)

PLATE 149
Detail of a robe (*attush*)
Aiushi (*thorned*) pattern
Plain-weave elm-bark fibre (*ohyō*) with cotton cloth appliqué and
embroidery in cotton thread
Hokkaidō; 19th century
T.99-1963
128.5 x 128 cm (50^1/$_2$ x 50^3/$_8$ in)
Leach Gift

PLATE 150
Page from a sample book of works by students of Kyoto Prefectural
Girl's School exhibited at the London International Health
Exhibition of 1884
Tea blossom
Relief work (*oshi-e*) in plain weave and crêpe (*chirimen*) silk
Kyoto; 1884
1080-1884
Sample: 22.5 x 19 cm (8^7/$_8$ x 7^1/$_2$ in)
Book: 24.5 x 30.5 cm (9^5/$_8$ x 12 in)

This piece of work was executed by 24-year-old Watanabe Teru, a
1st grade sewing student.

Plate 1. Sample (detail). t.100F-1969

PLATE 4. *Kimono* lining (detail). T.78-1927

38

PLATE 2. Sample (detail). T.100Q-1969

PLATE 3. Sample mounted in an album (detail). T.172-1963

PLATE 5. Length (detail). 333a-1865

PLATE 6. Length (detail). 330-1865

PLATE 7. Lining of a Buddhist priest's mantle (*kesa*, detail). T.86-1927

42

PLATE 10. Court robe (*kariginu*, detail). FE.157-1983

PLATE 11. Sample (detail). 1407-1899

PLATE 12. Length (detail). 83a-1884

44

PLATE 13. Sample (detail). 784.85-1884

Plate 14. Cover of a textile sample book (detail). T.63-1948

Plate 15. Sample (detail). 784.2-1884

PLATE 17. *Kimono* (detail). T.78-1927

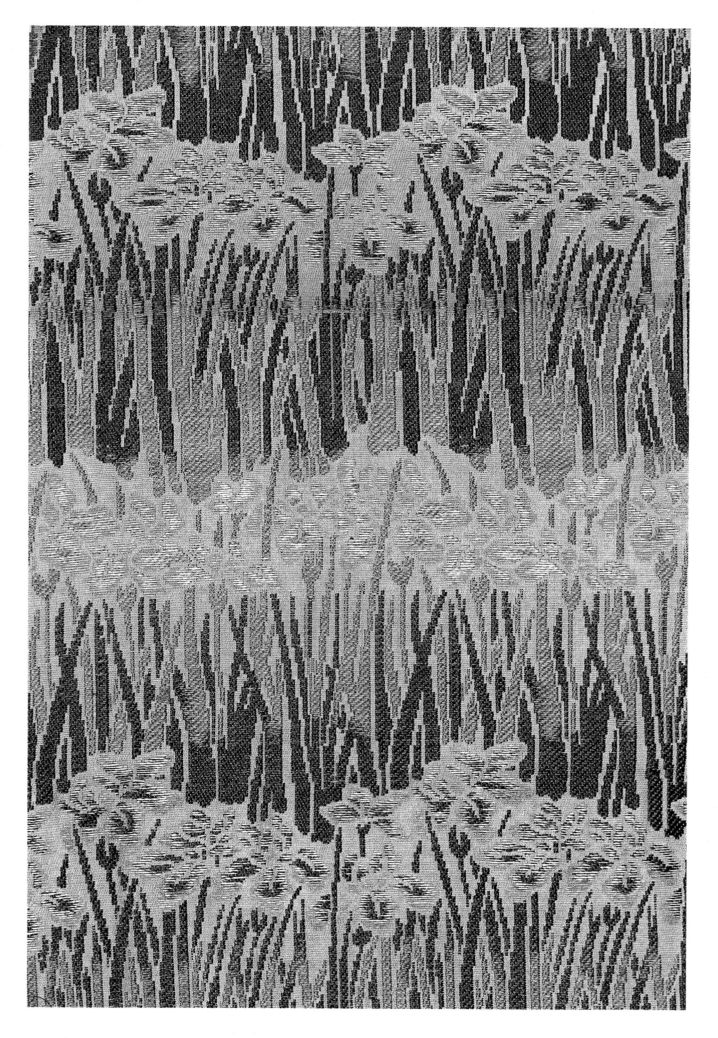

PLATE 16. Sample (detail). 751-1905

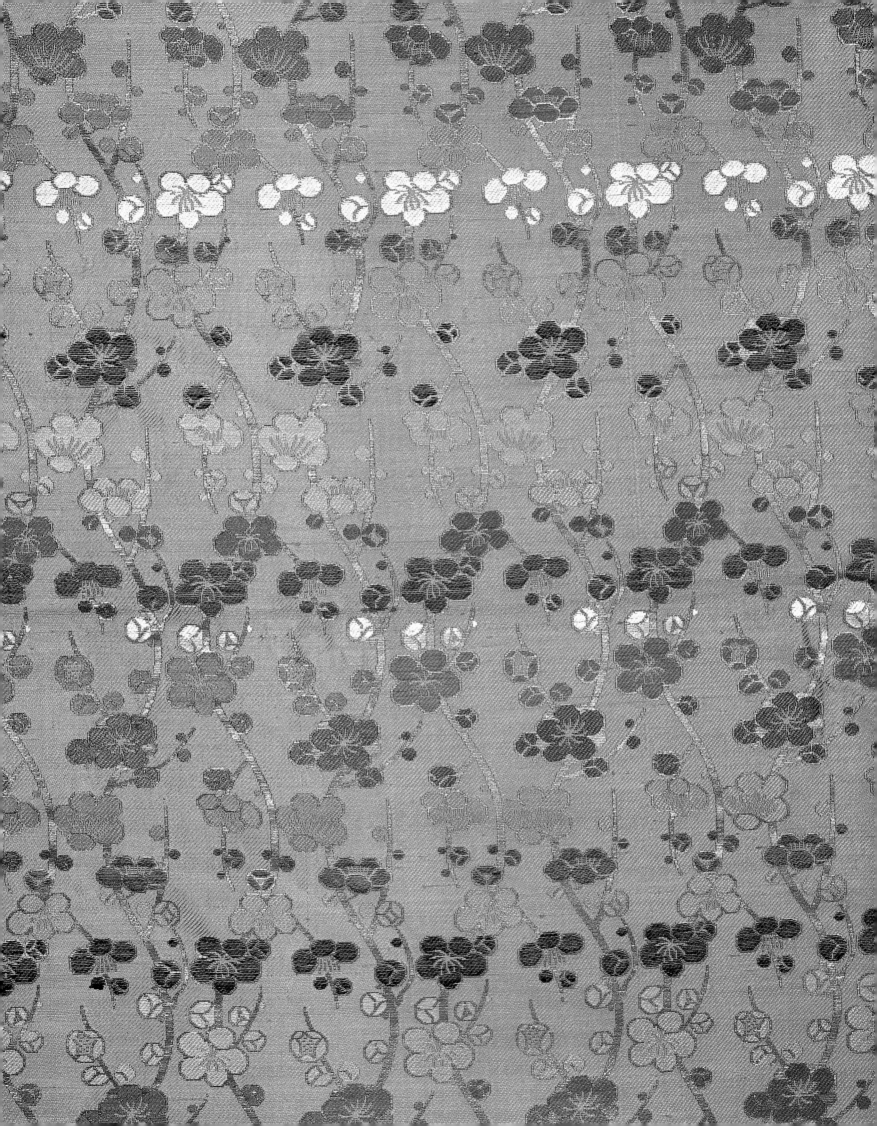

48

Plate 18. *Kimono* (detail). t.65-1915   Plate 19. *Obi* (detail). t.85-1927

PLATE 20. Length of *obi* fabric (detail). T.208-1934

PLATE 21. Length of *obi* fabric (detail). T.332-1970

PLATE 22. Thigh protector (*haidate*) from a suit of armour (detail). M.52.5-1909

PLATE 23. Sleeve (*kote*), possibly for mounted archery (detail). M.36a-1932

51

PLATE 24. Surcoat (*jimbaori*, detail). 628-1905

52

PLATE 25. *Nō robe (kariginu)*. FE.8-1984

PLATE 26. *Nō robe* (*atsuita*, detail). T.49-1915

PLATE 27. *Nō robe* (*karaori*, detail). T.194-1959

PLATE 28. Panel made from a *Nō* robe (*karaori*, detail). T.46-1955

PLATE 29. *Nō robe* (*atsuita*, detail). T.297-1963

PLATE 30. Length, possibly for a theatrical costume (detail). 319a-1865

56

PLATE 31. Jacket (*hitatare*), possibly for *Kyōgen* (detail). FE.69-1984

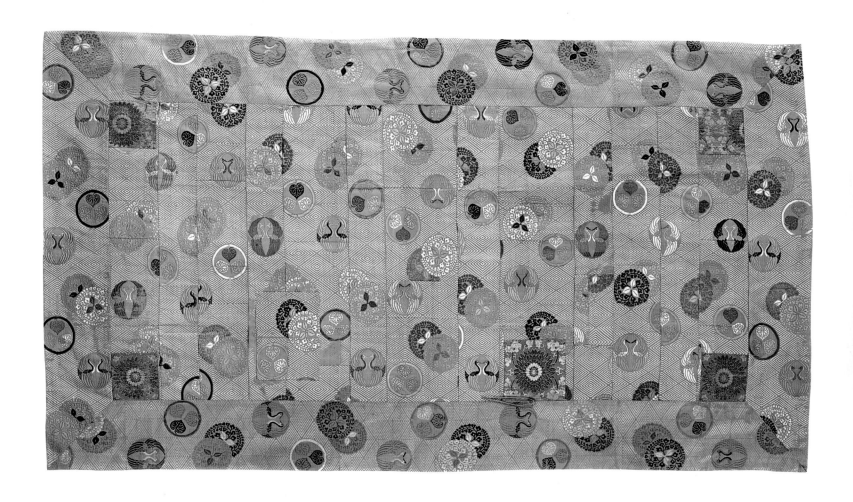

Plate 32. Buddhist priest's mantle (*kesa*). T.140-1927

58

PLATE 33. Buddhist priest's mantle (*kesa*, detail). T.84-1927

PLATE 34. Buddhist priest's mantle (*kesa*, detail). T.86-1927

PLATE 35. Buddhist priest's mantle (*kesa*, detail). T.80-1927

PLATE 36. Buddhist textile (detail). T.92-1927

PLATE 37. Buddhist textile (detail). T.93-1927

PLATE 38. Buddhist textile (detail). Circ.157-1927

62

PLATE 39. Buddhist textile (detail). T.88-1927

PLATE 40. Hanging from a Buddhist temple (detail). T.98-1927

64

PLATE 41. Hanging (detail). T.161-1969

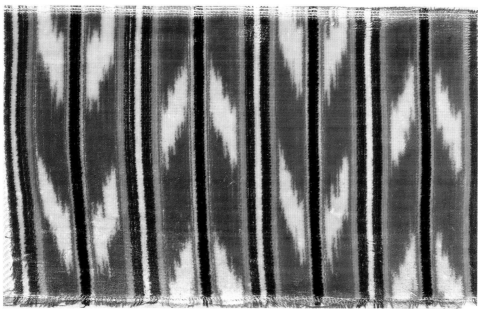

PLATE 43. Sample mounted in an album (detail). T.177-1953

66

PLATE 45. Hanging scroll. 1712-1888   PLATE 46. Hanging scroll (detail). 1709-1888

PLATE 47. Picture. T.104-1971

PLATE 48. Length (detail). T.110-1957

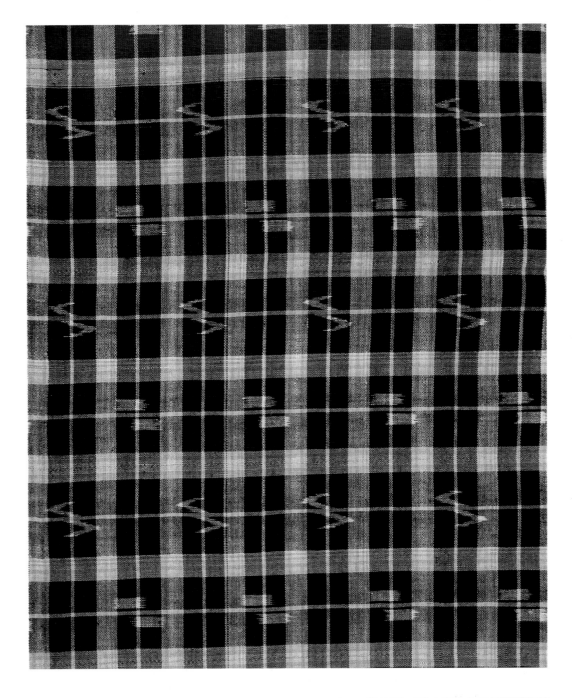

68

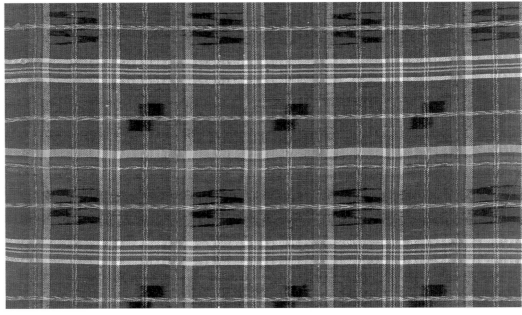

PLATE 49. Sample mounted in an album (detail). T.142-1968

PLATE 50. Bedding cover (*futon-ji*, detail). T.326-1960

PLATE 51. Bedding cover (*futon-ji*, detail). T.98-1969

PLATE 52. Sample. T.126-1968

PLATE 53. Length (detail). T.99-1957

PLATE 56. Length (detail). AP.43.3-1876

72

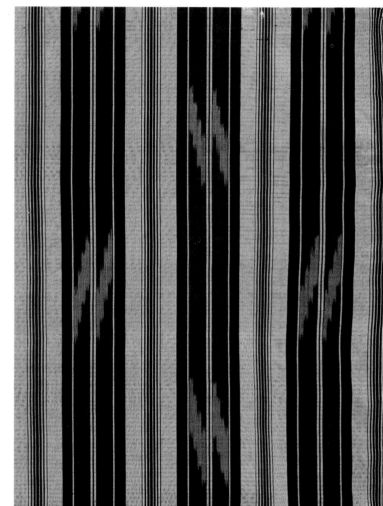

PLATE 54. *Kimono* (detail). T.329-1960

PLATE 55. *Kimono* for a child (detail). FE.51-1982

PLATE 57. Length (detail). AP.43.6-1876

PLATE 58. Page from a sample book. T.55-1957

PLATE 59. Coat (*michiyuki*, detail). FE.23-1989

PLATE 60. *Kimono* (detail). FE.162-1988

76

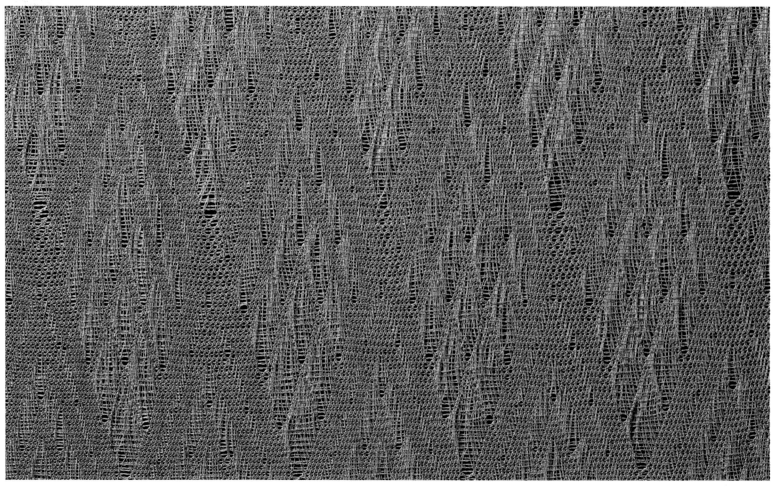

PLATE 63. *Puffed Blocks* (detail). By Arai Jun'ichi (b.1932). T.148-1990

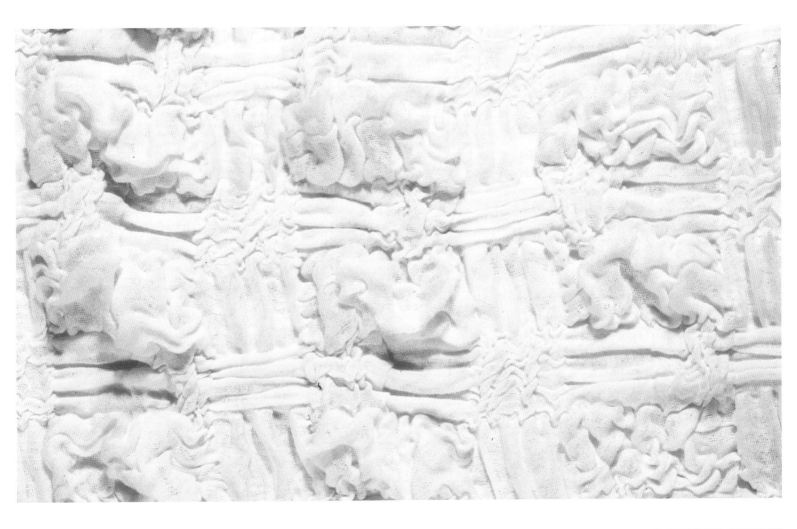

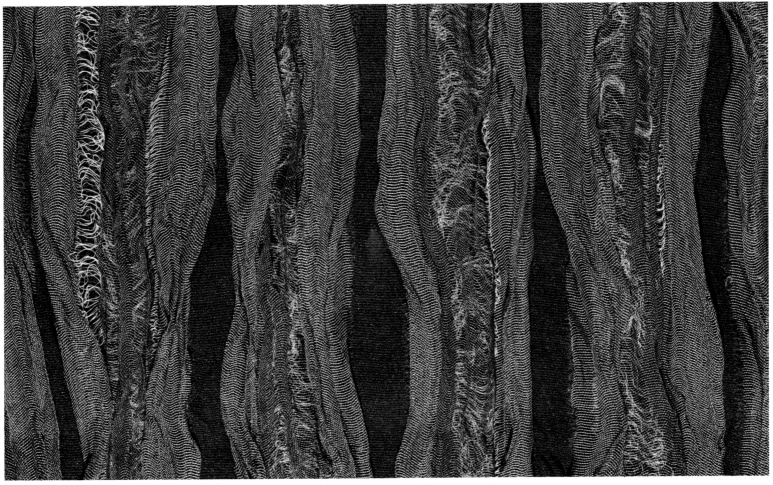

PLATE 64. *Seaweed Scarf* (detail). By Miyamoto Eiji (b.1948). FE.282-1995

PLATE 65. *Kimono* fragment (detail). 1588-1899

PLATE 66. *Kimono* (detail). T.109-1954

PLATE 67. *Kimono* (detail). FE.32-1982

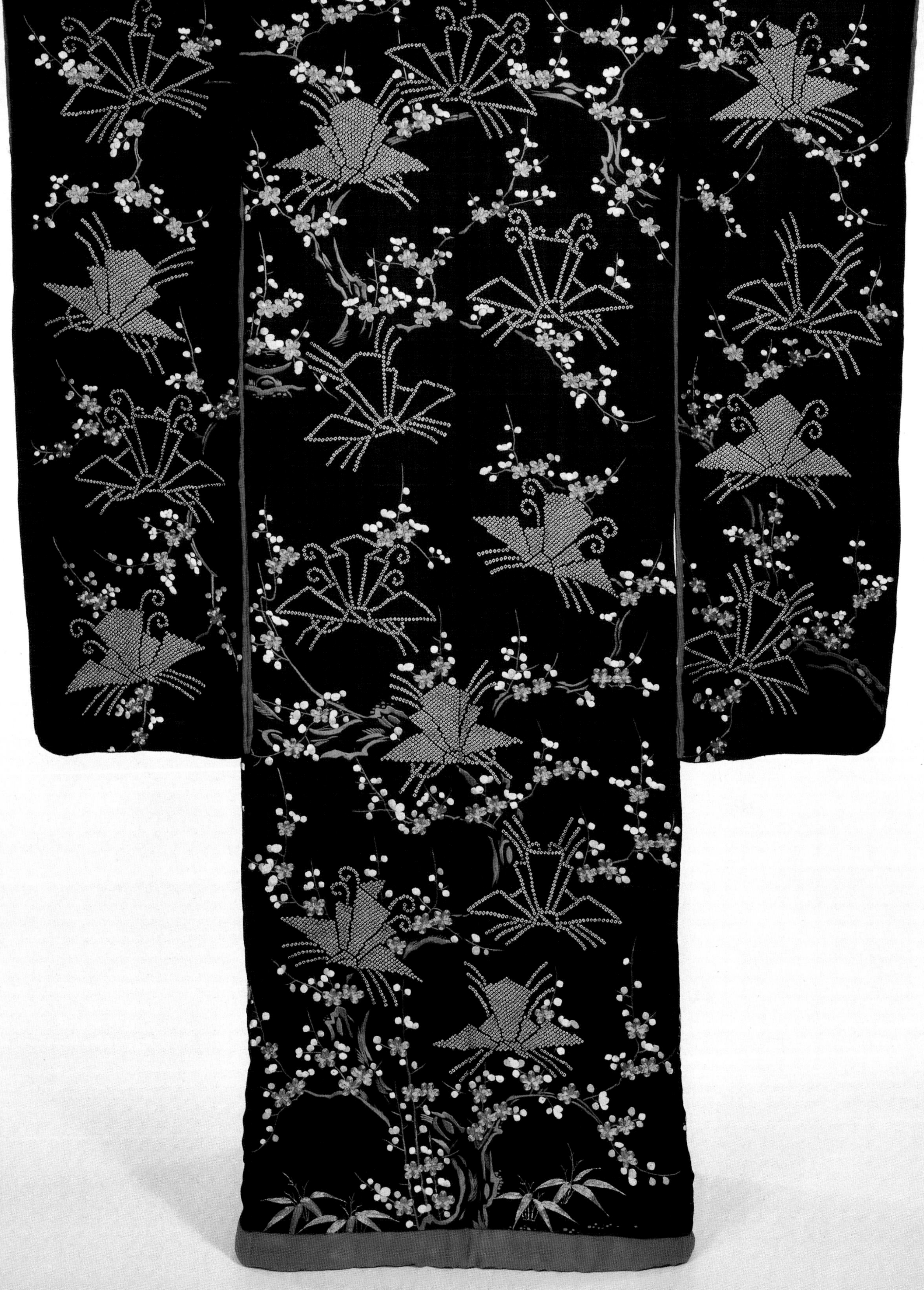

PLATE 68. *Kimono*. FE.28-1984

PLATE 69. *Kimono* (detail). FE.17-1994

82

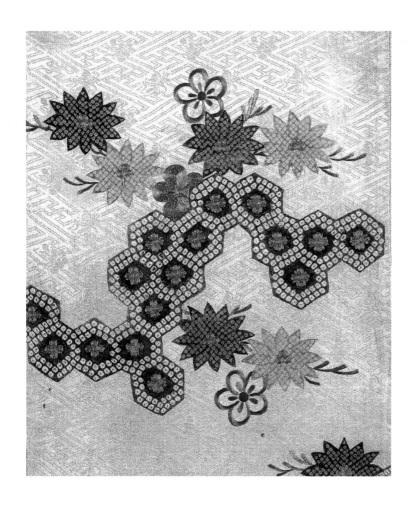

PLATE 70. *Kimono* (detail). FE.13-1983

PLATE 71. *Kimono* (detail). FE.8-1987

PLATE 72. *Kimono* (detail). FE.106-1982

PLATE 73. Pleated shoulder of a *samurai* jacket (*kataginu*, detail). FE.46-1980

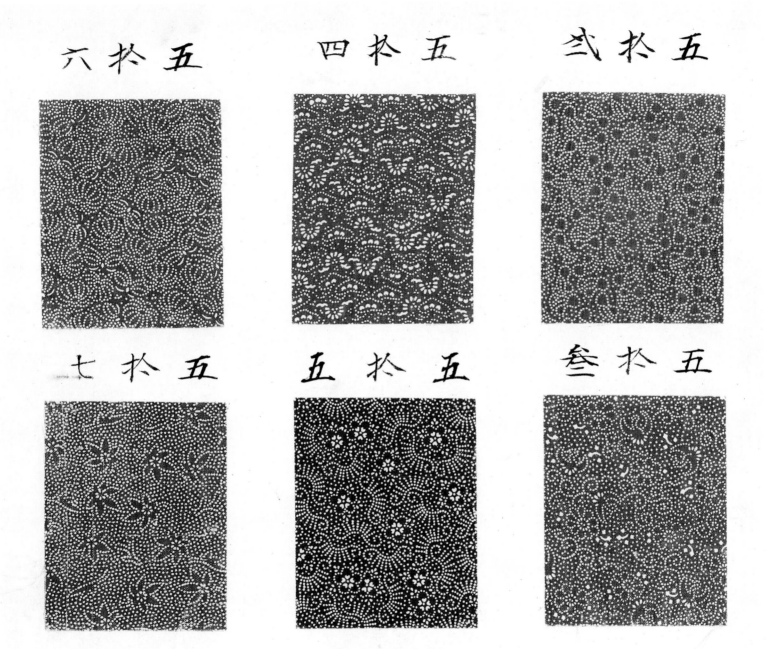

PLATE 74. Page of a sample book. T.150-1959

86

PLATE 75. Bedding cover (*futon-ji*, detail). FE.113-1997

PLATE 76. Fisherman's celebratory robe (*maiwai*, detail). FE.102-1982

PLATE 77. Sleeping coverlet (*yogi*, detail). FE.155-1983

PLATE 78. Robe (detail). T.18-1963

88

PLATE 79. Robe (detail). T.295-1960

PLATE 80. Robe (detail). FE.7-1983

Plate 83. Bedding cover (*futon-ji*), adapted from a sleeping coverlet (*yogi*). t.332-1960

PLATE 84. Bedding cover (*futon-ji*, detail). T.199-1964

PLATE 85. Festival banner, used as the backing of a temple hanging (detail). T.132-1927

PLATE 86. Doorway curtain (*noren*, detail). FE.49-1982

92

Plate 87. Length (detail). t.136-1968

Plate 88. Length (detail). t.137-1968

PLATE 89. Summer *kimono* (*katabira*, detail). T.17-1963

PLATE 90. Sample mounted in an album. T.50-1935

PLATE 91. Sample mounted in an album. T.175-1953

PLATE 92. Sample mounted in an album. T.49-1935

PLATE 93. *Kimono* section (detail). 79-1884

PLATE 94. *Kimono* (detail). 874-1891

PLATE 95. *Kimono* (detail). T.266-1968

PLATE 96. *Kimono* (detail). T.155-1965

PLATE 97. Length (detail). 842-1869

PLATE 98. *Kimono* (detail). FE.29-1987

PLATE 99. Gift cover (*fukusa*). T.260-1959

PLATE 100. Length (detail). T.429-1912

PLATE 101. *Kimono* (detail). FE.233-1974

PLATE 102. *Kimono* (detail). FE.12-1983

PLATE 103. Summer *kimono* (*katabira*, detail). T.87-1968

Plate 104. Jacket (*haori*, detail). FE.163-1988

Plate 105. *Kimono* (detail). FE.67-1997

PLATE 106. Page from sample book. FE.21-1997

PLATE 107. Page from sample book. FE.18-1997

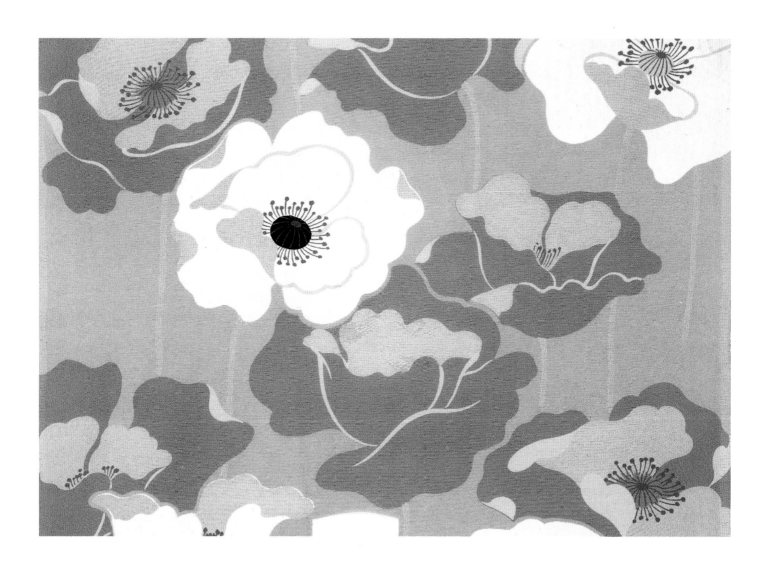

PLATE 108. Page from sample book. FE.18-1997

PLATE 109. Page from sample book. FE.22-1997

PLATE 110. Under*kimono* (*juban*, detail). FE.14-1987

108

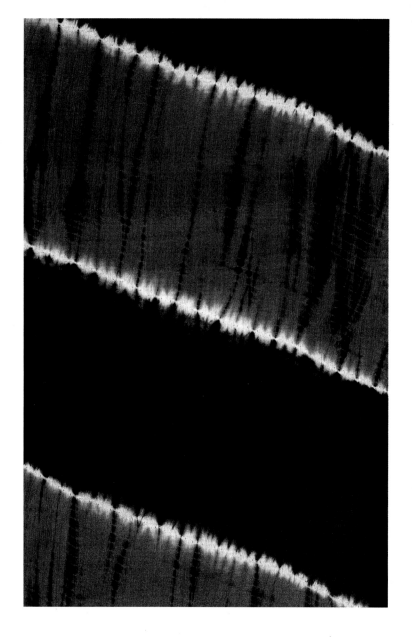

PLATE 111. Under*kimono* (*juban*, detail). FE.15-1987   PLATE 112. Jacket (*haori*, detail). FE.128-1988

PLATE 113. *Kimono* (detail). FE.127-1988

PLATE 114. Page from sample book. FE.25-1997

110

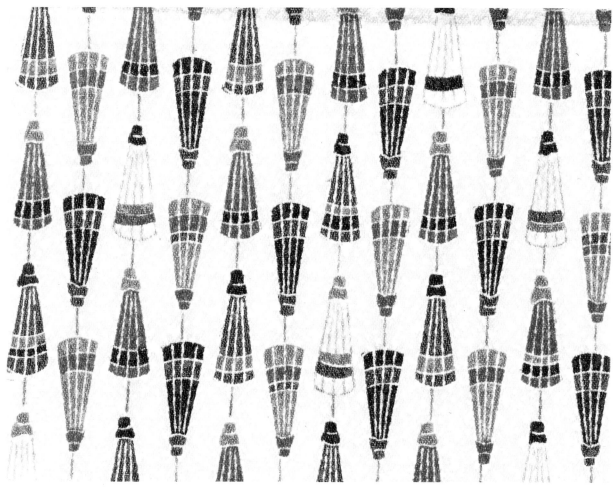

PLATE 115. Page from sample book. FE.23-1997

PLATE 116. Screen showing the stages of paper making (detail).
By Serizawa Keisuke (1895–1984). FE.20-1985

113

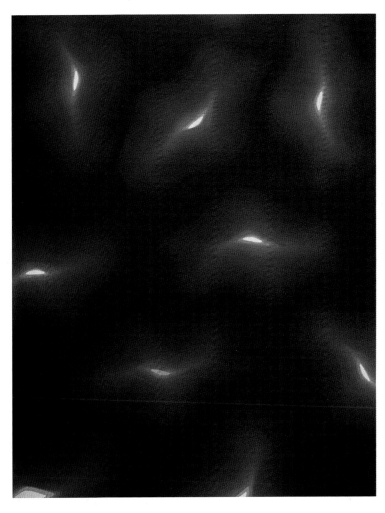

PLATE 118. *Kimono* entitled *Green Waves* (detail). By Moriguchi Kunihiko (b.1941).
FE.420-1992

PLATE 119. *Kimono* entitled *Flight* (detail). By Matsubara Yoshichi (b.1937).
FE.10-1995

PLATE 120. *Kimono* (detail). T.269-1960

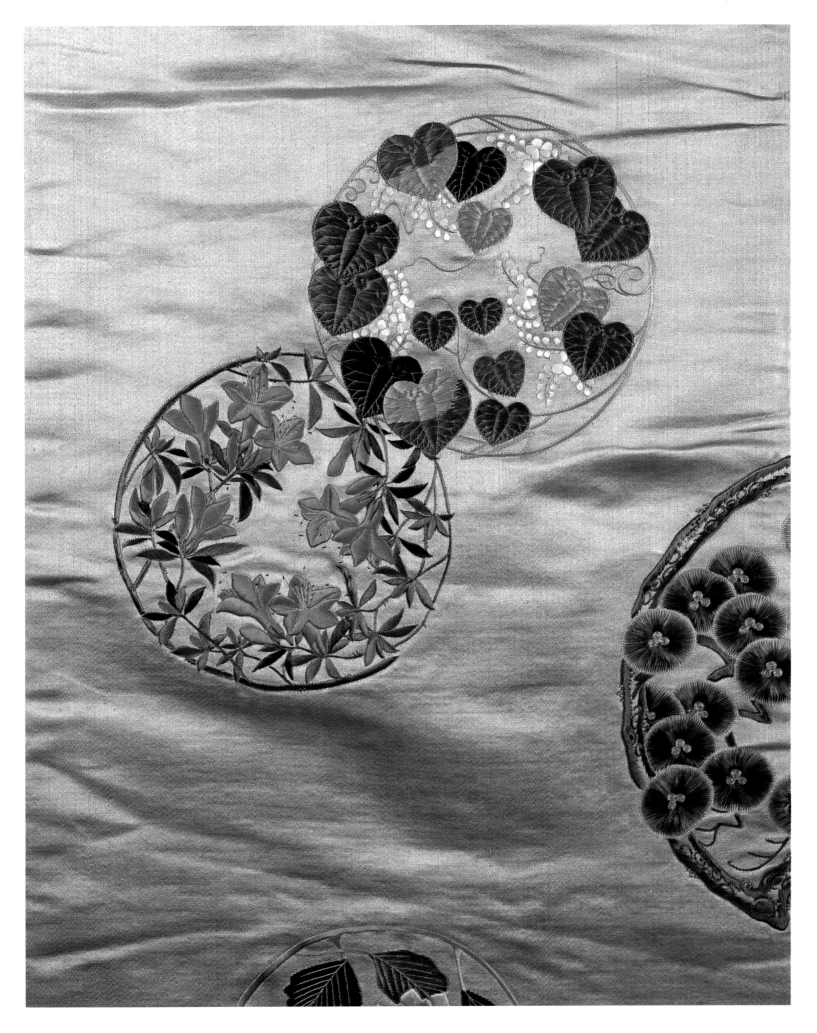

Plate 121. *Kimono* (detail). FE.11-1983

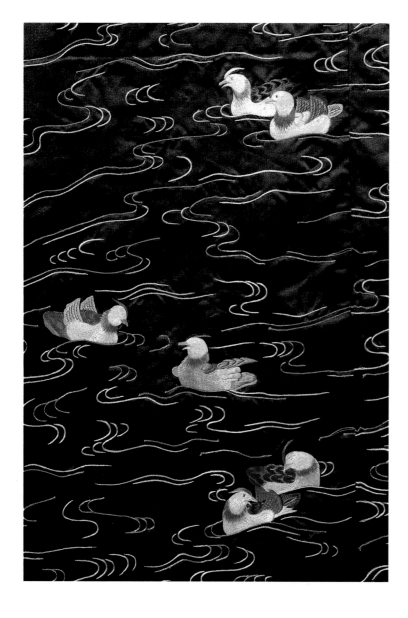

PLATE 122. *Kimono* (detail). FE.28-1987

PLATE 123. *Kimono* (detail). T.79-1927

PLATE 124. *Kimono* (detail). FE.36-1981

PLATE 125. *Kimono* (detail). T.72-1957

PLATE 126. *Kimono* (detail). T.178-1967

PLATE 127. *Obi* (detail). FE.23-1973

PLATE 128. *Obi* (detail). T.270-1960

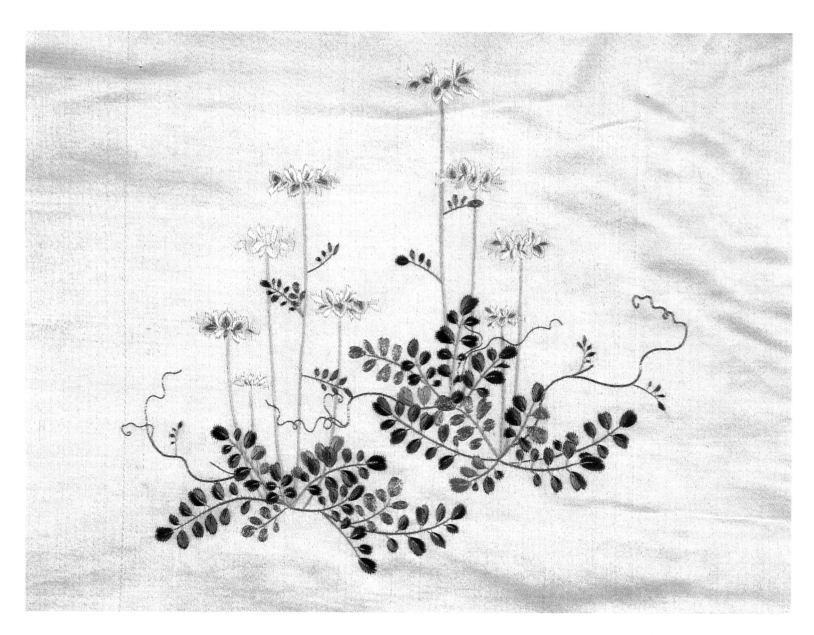

PLATE 129. Gift cover (*fukusa*, detail). Circ.169-1927

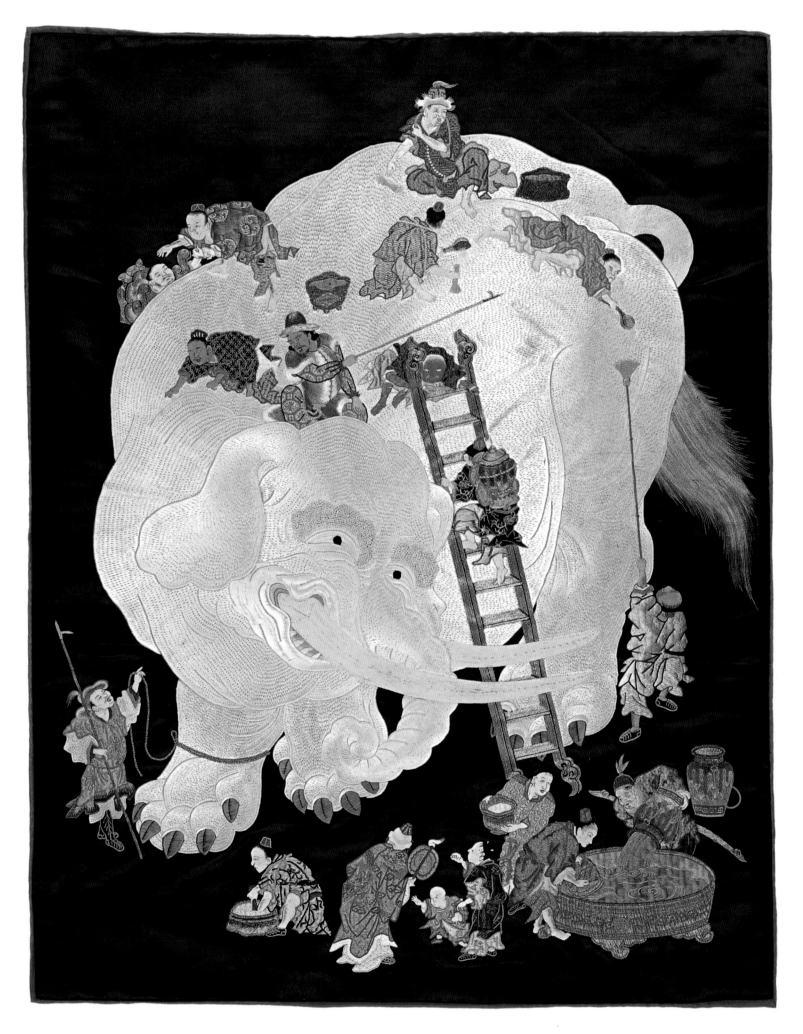

PLATE 130. Gift cover (*fukusa*). T.94-1927

PLATE 131. Gift cover (*fukusa*, detail). T.236-1967

PLATE 132. Gift cover (*fukusa*, detail). T.20-1923

PLATE 133. Gift cover (*fukusa*, detail). T.47-1910

PLATE 134. Gift cover (*fukusa*, detail). T.197-1963

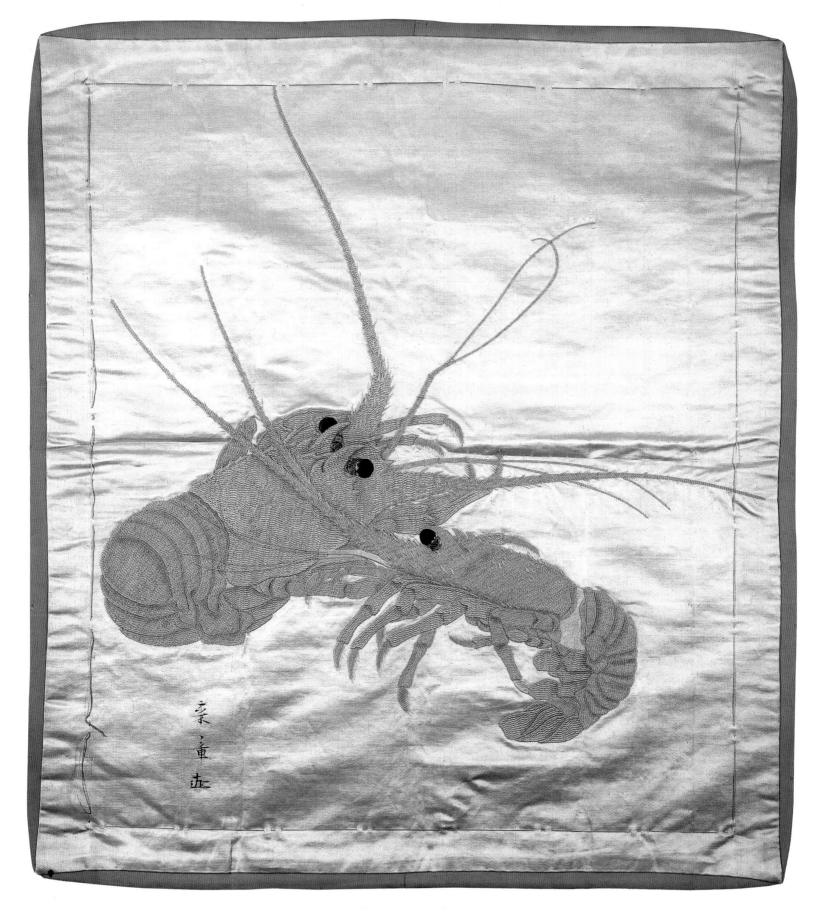

PLATE 135. Gift cover (*fukusa*). 81-1884

PLATE 136. Hanging from a Buddhist temple. T.208-1958

PLATE 137. Buddhist textile (detail). T.97-1927

PLATE 138. Buddhist textile (detail). Circ.167-1927

132

Plate 139. Buddhist textile (detail). t.96-1927

PLATE 141. Hanging, possibly from a Buddhist temple. T.252-1921

PLATE 142. Hanging from the Chio-in Temple, Kyoto (detail). 167-1898

PLATE 143. Hanging, possibly from a Buddhist temple (detail). T.94-1958

PLATE 144. Hanging. T.200-1968

PLATE 145. Hanging. T.5A-1911

PLATE 146. Page from a sample book of works by students of Kyoto Prefectural Girl's
School exhibited at the London International Health Exhibition of 1884. 1080-1884

PLATE 147. Work coat (detail). FE.30-1982

PLATE 148. *Kimono* (detail). FE.141-1983

PLATE 149. Robe (*attush*, detail). T.99-1963

BIBLIOGRAPHY

Brandon, Reiko M. *Bright and Daring: Japanese Kimono in the Taisho Mode* (Honolulu, Honolulu Academy of Art 1996)

Brandon, Reiko M. *Country Textiles of Japan: The Art Of Tsutsugaki* (New York and Tokyo, Weatherhill 1986)

Dalby, Liza. *Kimono: Fashioning Culture* (New Haven and London, Yale University Press 1993)

Earle, Joe, ed. *Japanese Art and Design* (London, Victoria & Albert Museum 1986)

Faulkner, Rupert. *Japanese Studio Crafts: Tradition and The Avant-Garde* (London, Laurence King 1995)

Gluckmann, Dale Carolyn and Sharon Sadako Takeda. *When Art Became Fashion: Kosode in Edo-Period Japan* (Los Angeles, Los Angeles County Museum of Art 1992)

Harris, Jennifer, ed. *5000 Years of Textiles* (London, British Museum Press 1993)

Hauser, William B. 'Textiles and Trade in Tokugawa Japan' in Maureen Fennell Mazzaoui, ed. *Textiles: Production, Trade and Demand* (Aldershot, Brookfield, Singapore and Sydney, Ashgate 1998)

Hay, Susan Anderson, ed. *Patterns and Poetry: Nō Robes from the Lucy Truman Aldrich Collection at the Museum of Art, Rhode Island School of Design* (Providence, Rhode Island, Museum of Art, Rhode Island School of Design 1992)

Jackson, Anna. *Japanese Country Textiles* (London and New York, Victoria & Albert Museum and Weatherhill 1997)

Japan Textile Colour Design Centre. *Textile Designs of Japan* (Tokyo and London, Kodansha and Serindia 1980), 3 vols

Kennedy, Alan. *Japanese Costume: History and Tradition* (Paris, Adam Biro 1990)

Liddell, Jill. *The Story of the Kimono* (New York, EP Dutton 1989)

McCarty, Clara and Matilda McQuaid. *Structure and Surface: Contemporary Japanese Textiles* (New York, The Museum of Modern Art 1998)

Robert Moes. *Mingei: Japanese Folk Art from the Montgomery Collection* (Alexandria, Virginia, Art Services International 1995)

Nakaoka, Tetsuro et al. 'The Textile History of Nishijin (Kyoto): East Meets West', *Textile History* (1988), vol. 19, no. 2, pp.117–42

Noma, Seiroku. *Japanese Costume and Textile Art* (Tokyo and New York, Heibonsha and Weatherhill 1974)

Rathbun, William Jay. *Beyond the Tanabata Bridge: Traditional Japanese Textiles* (New York, Thames and Hudson in association with the Seattle Art Museum 1993)

Stinchecum, Amanda Mayer. *Kosode: 16th–19th Century Textiles from the Nomura Collection* (New York, Kodansha and The Japan Society 1984)

Takemura, Akihiko. *Fukusa: Japanese Gift Covers* (Tokyo, Iwasaki Bijutsu-sha 1991)

Various Authors. *Kyoto Shoin's Art Library of Japanese Textiles* (Kyoto, Kyoto Shoin 1993–4), 20 vols

Woodson, Yoko et al. *Four Centuries of Fashion: Classical Kimono from the Kyoto National Museum* (San Francisco, The Asian Art Museum of San Francisco 1997)

Yamanobe, Tomoyuki and Kenzo Fujii. *Kyoto Modern Textiles* (Kyoto, Kyoto Textile Wholesalers Association 1996)